No Handle on the Cross

No Handle on the Cross

An Asian Meditation on the Crucified Mind

KOSUKE KOYAMA

[signature]

Pax christi

ORBIS ⊕ BOOKS

Maryknoll, New York 10545

1977

To the staff of the
Christian Conference of Asia

Library of Congress Cataloging in Publication Data

Koyama, Kosuke, 1929–
    No handle on the cross.

    1. Jesus Christ—Person and office—Addresses,
essays, lectures. 2. Christianity—Essence,
genius, nature—Addresses, essays, lectures.
3. Christian life—1960–   —Addresses, essays,
lectures. I. Title.
[BT202.K65]   232   76-23160
ISBN 0-88344-3384
ISBN 0-88344-3392 pbk.

Contents

Preface

This book is the outcome of the 1975 Earl Lecture which I was privileged to give at the Pacific School of Religion, California.

As a missionary of the United Church of Christ in Japan I taught theology at Thailand Theological Seminary in Chieng Mai, Thailand, from 1960 to 1968. My theological experiences in Thailand rekindled in me a love and respect for the Asian religious cultural heritages. I had the opportunity of working extensively with theological colleagues throughout South East Asia between 1968 and 1974 in connection with the Association of Theological Schools in South East Asia and the South East Asia Graduate School of Theology. The thoughts presented here have been with me since early in my ministry in South East Asia.

I believe that the crusading mind (I am using the term 'crusading' in a broad sense, referring to all kinds of 'crusading for ... ' and 'crusading against ... ') is a Christian mind if it is guided by the crucified mind. It is not the crusading mind but the crucified mind which will become the 'risen mind'. 'Jesus Christ crucified and risen ... ' And behind this observation an image is in my mind: 'No handle on the cross'.

1   Cross and Lunch-Box

Jesus Christ does not carry his cross as a businessman carries his briefcase.

Then Jesus told his disciples, 'If any man would come after me, let him deny himself and take up his cross and follow me ... ' (Matt.16.24). Jesus demands self-denial from us if we would come after him. The image of self-denial, given without any hesitation, is the cross. Self-denial must express itself through a socially recognizable symbol. What a thing to carry, of all things! What a heavy, badly-shaped, demoralizing object it is to take along as we follow him! Will it not slow down our pace? Will it not produce a persecution complex within us? Will it not make us too serious, too nervous, too sensitive, too emotional to fit into the normal run of every-day life? Picture the image of a man carrying the cross and following a man who goes ahead with his cross! What a procession! What a spectacle! 'I think that God has exhibited us apostles as last of all, like men sentenced to death; because we have become a spectacle to the world, to angels and to men' (I Cor.4.9). In following him, why is it necessary to take up a cross? In following him, why is the outward sign and inner mind to be a cross? Why not a lunch-box?

Why not a nourishing lunch-box in which are found boiled eggs (devilled eggs preferably), sliced Swiss cheese, a piece of New Zealand lamb chop and green lettuce and a thermos of hot coffee? How about such an 'over-developed, caloried-salaried, international, technological, carefully-packed lunch-box' for the sake of Jesus Christ? It is an attractively shaped box with a neat handle for carrying. It is not heavy. How psychologically and physically strengthening to carry such a lovely and substantial lunch-box! You know how our souls, let alone stomachs, are peacefully tranquil when our hands feel the comfortable weight of a lunch-box? Food is essential for any man. It must be essential in the matter of 'following him' too. How dare we follow Jesus with an empty stomach? Does not a Japanese proverb say that 'you cannot fight with an empty stomach'?

With a nourishing and well-filled lunch-box in our hands we can whistle and light-footedly follow Jesus 'from victory unto victory'. The lunch-box symbolizes our resourcefulness, spiritual and mental energy, high-powered substantial theology, good honest thinking, careful (international and technological) planning and sacred commitment to our faith. Why not, then, ' ... let him prepare himself and take up his lunch-box and follow me ... '? We can be and will remain energetic and resourceful. If necessary, we can even walk ahead of Jesus instead of 'follow him'.

The contrast is between the cross and the lunch-box: an extremely inconvenient thing to carry ('without a handle') and an extremely convenient thing to carry ('with a handle'); an ugly thing to carry and an attractive thing to carry; slow movement and fast movement; inefficiency and efficiency; insecurity and security; heavy-footedness and light-footedness; pain and glory; self-denial and self-assertion.

The cross does not have a handle. The lunch-box has a handle. May I invite you to meditate on this image? 'Handle' stands for a means of efficient control. Automobiles with powerful engines obey us because we control them through the handle (steering wheel). Doors can be efficiently controlled if we operate them by their handles. It is through switches that we control electric appliances of all kinds. Developed technological devices give us 'engines' (power) and 'handles' (control). Uncontrolled power is not technology. Technology is a controlled power. In that sense, it is not dangerous. In contrast, theology has a danger signal. The signal will be switched on if man yields to the strong temptation to 'control' God. The prayer of King Solomon, 'Behold, heaven and the highest heaven cannot contain thee' (II Chron. 6.18), represents a right theological perception. The basic difference between technology and theology is that the former gives us both an 'engine' and a 'handle', whereas the latter has an 'engine' but no 'handle'. Theology that puts a handle to the power of God is no longer a theology but a demonic theological ideology. Theology must refuse to 'handle' the saving power of God. It tries to speak about it. It tries to sing 'Magnificat' about it. It meditates about it. But it does not 'handle' it as we handle our car or washing machine. Theology, then, must not 'handle' people either.

The technological mind is, in short, 'handle-minded', while the theological mind is 'non-handle-minded'. Technology aims to control physical power. Theology does not aim to control the power of God. Theology, then, must not be approached with technological 'handle-mindedness'. It is said that in the India of ancient Vedic times one of the reasons for the ascendancy of the Brahmin priestly class in the community was their claim that they alone knew how to officiate in elaborate sacrificial rites to appease and control the gods. There is a touch of technological handle-mindedness here. I notice the presence of such a mind in the prayer: 'God, I thank thee that I am not like other men, extortioners, unjust, adulterers, or even like this tax collector. I fast twice a week, I give tithes of all that I get' (Luke 18.11,12).

The mind which is trained under the weight of the cross 'without a handle' is called the crucified mind. The mind which is trained in carrying 'essential resourcefulness' 'with a handle' is called the crusading mind. The Pharisaic prayer makes a contrast to the prayer of the tax collector: 'God, be merciful to me a sinner.' I do not intend to reject the crusading mind. The lunch-box-carrying crusading mind must be carefully and kindly dealt with in the community of faith. I believe that it has a God-given role to play in our mission. But I maintain that the crusading mind must not function by itself. It must be guided and illuminated by the crucified

How to carry this bulky, heavy
and demoralizing thing?

Does Jesus carry the cross as a
businessman carries his
briefcase?

How easy and encouraging it
is to carry a neat well-packed
lunch-box 'with a handle'!

mind. The life-style of the Pharisee is commendable. The
religious dedication and spiritual resourcefulness of the
Pharisee are of high value. 'Unless your righteousness exceeds
that of the scribes and Pharisees, you will never enter the
kingdom of heaven' (Matt. 5.20). His theological lunch-box is
full of high-protein foods. The famous parable ends, however,
with this devastating conclusion: 'I tell you, this man (the tax
collector) went down to his house justified rather than the
other (the Pharisee).' Does not this mean that such a
dedicated religious and spiritual resourcefulness as the
Pharisee exhibited is unable to create the right kind of
relationship with his God and with his fellow-men? Why is the
Pharisee's dedication misguided? Why is the world today, in
every area of human existence, full of the tragedy of mutilated
resourcefulness? Why does not the New Testament draw a

quick and assuring connection line between justification and resourcefulness?

The crusading mind must be placed in the light of the crucified mind in order to be 'crucified and risen'. I understand this to be the reason why Jesus did not say ' ... let him assert himself and take up his lunch-box and follow me'. Resourcefulness (that over-developed lunch-box) must be theologically judged and contextualized in order to become genuinely resourceful. Resourcefulness must then be crucified. When it is resurrected it will become a 'theologically-baptized resourcefulness'. Asian church history is telling us today that often missionaries' resourcefulness has resulted in the impoverishment of native participation in the mission of God. Resourceful persons do not seek help from others. They know exactly what to do. They have 'better ideas'. They have 'better strategies'. 'God, I thank thee that I am not like other men who are not resourceful ... ' In the perspective of mission together in the six continents we urgently need ecumenical meditation on the theology of crucified resourcefulness.

I wish to say a few words about crucified resourcefulness. Have you heard about the 'moratorium debate' in the Christian mission? It is one of the most critical mission problems facing the churches in Asia, Africa and Latin America today. A moratorium is,

> the cessation of presently existing support in personnel and funds and the delay of any new support 'for a reasonable length of time' to allow review and possible revision of the best use of persons and money in response to God's mission and the churches' search for selfhood in this day and in this world. Behind this objective lay the conviction that past patterns of domination and dependence, both secular and ecclesiastical, inhibited rather than enhanced the response to God's mission in both 'sending' and 'receiving' churches ... [1]

I am convinced of the need of moratorium. I have seen the crippling effects upon the indigenous churches' sense of responsibility in the traditional system of mission. True, the issue is a complicated one. In spite of our sincerity and dedication, the fact is that both the sending and the receiving churches have suffered spiritually and organizationally in tragic proportion. The moratorium proposal is directed at the ills of the present mission *system*. The churches in Asia have not had their own 'family time'. Does not any family need to be left alone at least once a while (once in a hundred years!) to do their own domestic work by their own judgment and resourcefulness, so that they can see clearly where they are and who they are in relation to their own mission? Or must a family be constantly visited and surrounded by the 'love and care' of another family? The Church of Christ in Thailand is one family. It is more than 150 years old in terms of Christian life. Don't they need time to work out their own Christian responsibility on the basis of their *own* 'five barley loaves and two fishes'? Moratorium expresses a desire on the part of the churches in Asia to be temporarily free from the 'constant love and care' of the Western church. The risen Lord does *not* say 'Go therefore and stay for ever ... ' (Matt. 28.19). Our resourcefulness both in the West and in Asia must receive careful theological examination. It must be crucified in order to be risen. Ogbu U. Kalu writes that planting '*ecclesia anglicana* in Africa is loaded with contradictions. It is obvious that there is no way to realize what the Kingdom of God means on African soil and to awaken people to abundant life in the incarnation and ministry of Christ with such foreign institutions and others like it. They must be destroyed in order to build the new'.[2] Our mission vision and system must be crucified in order to be risen.

Let me now go back to the image of Jesus Christ. The image of Jesus under the weight of the bulky and *handleless* cross is a pregnant missiological image in the light of which the theological meaning of our every-day Asian situation must be sought. Such an image as Jesus carrying a cross in the same way that an American businessman in Hong Kong carries a briefcase is theologically sterile and missiologically abhorrent.

We can shave Jesus. We can put a necktie on Jesus. We can put a pair of glasses over his eyes and a Sony transistor radio in his hands. We can even place a colourful Diners Card in his hands (?!). But if you put a handle on his cross so that he can carry it as a businessman carries a briefcase, then the Christian faith has lost its ground. Theology is then paralysed. Christian ethics has lost its inner inspiration. Such a Jesus who carries his cross as one carries a briefcase – ultimately this points to the God who carries the world around as one carries a briefcase – brings a fatal heart-attack to the Christian faith. No matter how elaborate, fascinating, efficient and resourceful it may be, the theology of such a Jesus cannot be true to the saving message and the mode of salvation given in the biblical tradition. In the Bible, the cross does not have a 'handle'. Let me emphasize that for me the image of Jesus carrying over his shoulders the intolerable weight of the bulky cross – he did not know how to carry it, yet he carried it 'without a handle' – is the primary image for the understanding and explication of the Christian truth urgently needed today in Asia.

The profoundly touching revelation of the inner feeling of God in Hosea, ch.11, includes this well-known verse: 'I led them with cords of compassion (NEB 'leading-strings'), with the bands of love (NEB 'bonds of love' or 'reins of hide'), and I became to them as one who eases the yoke on their jaws, and I bent down to them and fed them' (v.4). In spite of linguistic ambiguities, the spirit of the image is that of 'cords of compassion and bonds of love' which is placed in the context of God who 'bent down (an undesirable posture, technologically speaking) to them and fed them'. God does not come to man with 'handle-mindedness'. I subject the image of lunch-box carrying to this primary image. The latter is closer to the mind of God and the mind of man than the former. It is the mind of Jesus Christ who, in his mystery, upholds history.

2 The Mind Captivated by the 'Foolishness and Weakness of God'

> The crucified mind is a shaken mind that feels the power of God coming from the crucified Lord.
>
> Jesus Christ deepens human situations while he bends down.
>
> The crucified mind is not a sickly mind.

When I speak of the crucified mind I am thinking of the crucified Lord. If I were to speak about the crucified mind apart from my faith in the crucified Lord, I would be advocating some neurotic persecution complex. 'I decided to know nothing among you except Jesus Christ and him crucified', declares Paul (I Cor. 2.2). 'Cross, worthy to be loved, in whom is our salvation, our life, and resurrection' (Anselm). ' "The Gospel of the cross" can be interpreted in many meaningful ways. But its central thrust is found in the truth that Christ achieves victory through accepting defeat' (Kanzo Uchimura). The mind which has decided to live by the power of the crucified Lord is the crucified mind. The mind which desires to seek understanding through the wisdom of the crucified Lord is the crucified mind. It is the mind that speaks of Jesus Christ through the influence of the spirituality and mentality of the crucified Lord.

I would like to invite you to I Corinthians 1.18-25. It is here that the crucified mind prominently suggests itself.

> For the word of the cross is folly to those who are perishing, but to us who are being saved it is the power of God.

The message of the cross comes to us and shakes our spirituality and mentality. Those who are shaken cannot but feel the power of God. This shaken mind is the crucified mind.

Thus the crucified mind is not in the first instance a wisdom mind, a philosophical mind or a religious mind. It is a shaken mind that feels the power of God coming from the crucified Lord.

> For it is written, 'I will destroy the wisdom of the wise, and the cleverness of the clever I will thwart'. Where is the wise man? Where is the scribe? Where is the debater of this age? Has not God made foolish the wisdom of the world?

What a strong saying! Will God destroy all wisdom in the history of man regardless? Does this mean that the wisdom of the Buddha, the Enlightened One, will be destroyed? Does this mean that the wisdom of Confucius and Mencius will be destroyed? Or does this mean that the wisdom that rejects the wisdom of the cross will be destroyed? Have the sages rejected, then, the wisdom of the cross? When does one reject the crucified Lord? Is Jesus Christ as easily rejected as is a poorly made children's toy at a toy shop? The crucified mind believes that Jesus Christ, the utterly rejected, cannot be so easily rejected by man!

> For since, in the wisdom of God, the world did not know God through wisdom, it pleased God through the folly of what we preach to save those who believe.

Believing is more than understanding. Believing is more than affirming. 'I believe; help my unbelief!' (Mark 9.24). To believe in the crucified Lord, saying that he is the victor and that in him is life's meaning and hope, is the life-beat of the crucified mind. The crucified mind involves intensive spirituality. It is so strongly focused on the crucified Lord that it invites serious misunderstanding: 'We are treated as impostors, and yet are true; as unknown, and yet well known; as dying, and behold we live; as punished, and yet not killed; as sorrowful, yet always rejoicing; as poor, yet making many rich; as having nothing, and yet possessing everything' (II Cor. 6.8-10). This is the life-style given to the crucified mind. It is to live with this possibility of grave misunderstanding.

There is no way of proving that the apostolic mind is the truthful mind and not a defrauding mind. The crucified mind receives inspiration from the apostolic mind. It tries to demonstrate its power (I Cor. 4.20) by believing in the crucified Lord and crucifying 'proofs' to show that it is true.

> For Jews demand signs and Greeks seek wisdom, but we preach Christ crucified, a stumbling block to Jews and folly to Gentiles, but to those who are called, both Jews and Greeks, Christ the power of God and wisdom of God. For the foolishness of God is wiser than men, and the weakness of God is stronger than men.

The crucified mind is not a proof-sign-seeking mind. It is not a speculative-wisdom-seeking mind. Both 'signs' and 'wisdom' have substantial histories within the spiritual experience of man. But in the context of the apostolic preaching Jesus Christ is the Sign and Wisdom *given* to man. Proof-signs and speculation-wisdom are overshadowed by the living presence of Jesus Christ in whom the church has its foundation. The crucified Lord judges proof-theology and speculation-theology. He judges them not cheaply but in a costly way as the one who is crucified. The crucified Lord, if he is presented as crucified, will remain 'a stumbling block to Jews and folly to Gentiles'. The crucified Lord demonstrates 'the foolishness of God' (!) which is wiser than men, and 'the weakness of God'(!) which is stronger than men. The immensely costly foolishness! The immensely saving weakness! To know this always, to try to understand this always, to be guided by this always, and constantly to train oneself to appreciate this 'foolishness and weakness of God' is the secret joy and strength of the crucified mind. The crucified mind is the mind shaken by the 'foolishness and weakness of God'.

There is an intriguing story in the Gospel of John (7.53-8.11; other ancient authorities add this story at the end of the gospel or after Luke 21.38).

> They went each to his own house, but Jesus went to the Mount of Olives. Early in the morning he came again to the

temple; all the people came to him, and he sat down and taught them. The scribes and the Pharisees brought a woman who had been caught in adultery, and placing her in the midst they said to him, 'Teacher, this woman has been caught in the act of adultery, Now in the law Moses commanded us to stone such. What do you say about her?' This they said to test him, that they might have some charge to bring against him. Jesus bent down and wrote with his finger on the ground. And as they continued to ask him, he stood up and said to them, 'Let him who is without sin among you be the first to throw a stone at her.' And once more he bent down and wrote with his finger on the ground. But when they heard it, they went away, one by one, beginning with the eldest, and Jesus was left alone with the woman standing before him. Jesus looked up and said to her, 'Woman, where are they? Has no one condemned you?' She said, 'No one, Lord.' And Jesus said, 'Neither do I condemn you: go, and do not sin again.'

This is another 'bent down' story. The story does far more than criticize the legalism of the scribes and the Pharisees. Jesus did not reject Moses. He deepened Moses. The profound intention of the ancient spiritual heritage of Israel was not violated, but truly realized. In this act of deepening, the position of Jesus was clear and simple; there is not a sign of abstruse discussion attached. He places one unmistakable preface of deepening on to the law of Moses. Indeed Moses was right! Let us follow his law. *But* let us not follow it with a crusading mind (the resourcefulness mind and the mind of efficient theology) but in the crucified mind ('I believe; help my unbelief!', Mark 9.24). 'Jesus bent down and wrote with his finger on the ground … ' as if he was calling the earth, the whole created world, to witness this event of deepening. ' … it is by the finger of God that I cast out demons … ' (Luke 11.20). While he 'bent down' (a 'foolish and weak' posture!), he prepared his deepening of the spiritual tradition of Moses and Israel.

Jesus did not condemn the scribes and the Pharisees. He upheld the *direction* of their theological intention. But his deepening brought forth a completely new theological situation, the one in which he could see 'Satan fall like lightning from heaven' (Luke 10.18). Jesus revealed the primal intention of God towards broken human situations. He did so by deepening the situation of adultery! 'Let him who is without sin among you be the first to throw a stone at her ... '

'Jesus looked up and said to her ... '. Jesus is speaking to her from the lower position, the position of being 'bent down'. 'Woman, where are they ... ?' She said, 'No one, Lord'. Jesus took her word. Jesus accepted the observation she made about the changed situation which he, not she, had brought about. She told Jesus simply what she saw had happened. On the basis of her observation (!) Jesus said simply: 'Neither do I condemn you; go, and do not sin again.' He overlooked all 'important theological questions'! Why did he say 'neither do I condemn you'? He did not give any reason for doing this. He deepened the situation and in his deepening he exercised his freedom. 'Neither do I condemn you' derives from 'bent-down theology'. The deepening words of Jesus generated a 'risen mind' within the woman. The woman was 'risen'. The resourceful crusading mind of the scribes and the Pharisees experienced crucifixion. By deepening it, Jesus healed the ugly situation. What a spiritual power had this man who 'bent down'! By deepening, not by 'handling'! 'For the foolishness of God is wiser than men, and the weakness of God is stronger than men.'

The crucified mind, then, is not a sickly mind. It is not suffering from a persecution complex. It is not a mutilated mind. It is not a business-transaction-with-God mind. It is not a paternalistic mind. It is a theologically inspired mind. It is an honest and careful mind. It is a believing mind. It is weak, yet a strong mind. It is foolish, yet a wise mind. It is the mind confessing 'I believe, help my unbelief!' Basically it is a mind of Jesus Christ who carried the cross 'without a handle', and prepared deepening while he was 'bent down'.

3   Without a Handle

God comes to history. He does not 'handle' history.
The hands of Jesus are painfully neither open nor closed.

I understand that the unique and enduring spiritual insight which the Judaeo-Christian tradition contributes to mankind is that the personal God, the one who creates, preserves and consummates all things, does not 'handle' history. He does not put a 'handle' to history in order to carry it around (with theological and technological speed!) as he pleases. He comes to history. He does not come to history with 'handle-mindedness'. He comes to history, to use an awkward expression, with a great respect for history. When he comes, history at its depth experiences the 'shaking of the foundation', because history has never been so profoundly and carefully taken up and respected. History has never been so profoundly penetrated and enlightened because of God's respectful approach to history. 'The true light that enlightens every man was coming into the world. He was in the world, and the world was made through him, yet the world knew him not' (John 1.9,10). 'The world knew him not'! Why? It is because God came to history but he did not handle history. The best of the Judaeo-Christian tradition is located in the historical spiritual energy which this theological insight has engendered.

I would like to speak of God's 'respectful' approach to history, 'without a handle', by means of two images: first, the image of God who said, 'Where are you?'; second, the image of the hands of Jesus.

(a) God said, 'Where are you?' (Gen. 3.9)

In the perspective of theology and ministry, this simple

question consisting of three words summarizes the history of
mankind, Israel and the church. This is so because in its
simple and forceful formulation, it points to the mode, the
method and the attitude of God towards history. 'Where are
you?' is a question 'without a handle', not a 'wise' question
and not a 'strong' question. It is therefore 'wiser' than all wise
questions, and 'stronger' than all strong questions. This
'weak' and 'foolish' question summarizes history not from the
top of Mount Olympus or Mount Fuji, but from the top of the
cross. ' ... I, when I am lifted up from the earth, will draw all
men to myself' (John 12.32). God's 'Where are you?',
addressed to man, is a promising theological insight with
which to approach the meaning of human life in history.

When the Creator (God who does not carry mankind as a
businessman carries his briefcase) said 'Where are you?' to
man, it meant that he decided to limit his 'where he is' by
man's 'where he is'. Thus, the question 'Where are you?' is a
revelation of the one who asks it. When God introduced
himself by making reference to three human names,
Abraham, Isaac and Jacob (Exod. 3.15), he revealed himself
and simultaneously identified the whereabouts of Abraham,
Isaac and Jacob. When he introduced himself, they were
introduced! This is salvation! Such a mind that seeks man is
the covenant-seeking and covenant-steadfast mind. God's
'Where are you?' is the expression of his commitment to man
at all costs. At all costs? Yes. Is not a non-handle approach to
history costly? Is not a non-handle approach to history
inefficient, slow and even agonizing? Is it not a 'weak' and
'foolish' approach? Do not the concepts of 'to have a handle'
and 'to be wise' go together? 'See, I have set you this day over
nations and over kingdoms, to pluck up and to break down, to
destroy and to overthrow, to build and to plant'. (Jer. 1.10).
Yet it is important to notice that such a powerful intention of
God is to be communicated to the world through young
Jeremiah, who does 'not know how to speak' (v.6). The words
of v.10 are not words of 'handle-mindedness'.

I would like to invite you to the first twelve chapters of

Genesis. These chapters give us the story of primeval history up to the call of Abraham. What I am intending to give is a brief sketch of God's 'non-handle' coming to primeval history. As we study the narrative of primeval history, we notice that there is a succession of serious outbreaks of sin and corresponding grace by God which makes an outline of 'non-handle theology'.

First comes the fall of man. Immediately after the act of disobedience 'the eyes of both were opened'. They were no longer in the state of primeval innocence. They began to have their own way of looking at things and themselves. They began to have their own theology. They became responsible to themselves. Their 'guiltless relation to God and to one another' (*Oxford Annotated Bible*) symbolized by their nakedness is destroyed. So they made fig-leaf aprons. (The textile industry has this theological dimension. A certain provocative use of the products of the textile industry points to the same theological truth from a negative angle.) God comes to them. 'Where are you?'

God replaces their fig-leaf aprons by the better quality 'garments of skins' (3.21). The primeval couple were judged (3.14-19), but they were 'helped' and 'respected'. God knew that the new context of civilization (outside-the-garden civilization) makes it necessary for man to wear more than a fig-leaf apron. God helps man to be adjusted to the new situation. 'Garments of skins' is a symbol of God's continuous concern for man who has become aware of his nakedness. When man becomes critically aware of his insecurity, his fig-leaf apron is replaced by God's garments of skins.

Then comes the murder of Abel by Cain. After the hideous crime, God comes to Cain with the question 'Where is Abel your brother?' God knows where Cain is and where Abel is. But Cain must answer responsibly where Abel is. 'Where is he?' asks far more than a locational answer. It means 'How is he?' Is your brother Abel enjoying šālôm (from the Akkadian root sălâmu – 'to be whole, uninjured') in his community life? 'Am I my brother's keeper?' says Cain. Since God has asked

the question, man must be asking the same question of his
neighbour. God's 'Where are you?' must produce man's
'Where are you?' to his neighbours in chain reaction. This
chain reaction has been radically disrupted by Cain. Cain
speaks to God with full awareness of his desperate situation:
'Behold, thou hast driven me this day away from the ground
and from thy face I shall be hidden' (4.14). Cain expresses his
feeling of terrible insecurity. It is physical ('away from the
ground') and theological ('from thy face I shall be hidden')
insecurity. Being forsaken by ground and God, Cain becomes
the most unprotected person on the face of the earth (4.14).
'Then the Lord said to him "Not so!" ' (v.15). *Not so!*

There follows the Song of Lamech. Lamech is a son of
Methushael, the son of Irad, the son of Enoch, and Enoch is
the son of Cain. Cain built a city and named it Enoch.
Lamech's wife Adah (his other wife's name is Zillah) bore
Jabal who became the father of cattle men. Jubal, the brother
of Jabal, was 'the father of all those who play the lyre and
pipe'. Tubal-cain, the son of Zillah, was the 'forger of all
instruments of bronze and iron'. In the line of Cain the
biblical writers (the Jahwist) place the origin of civilization. Is
it because all civilizations are not free from the shadow of
Cain? Here is the Song of Lamech:

> Lamech said to his wives; 'Adah and Zillah, hear my voice;
> you wives of Lamech, hearken to what I say: I have slain a
> man for wounding me, a young man for striking me. If Cain
> is avenged sevenfold, truly Lamech seventy-sevenfold'
> (4.23,24).

This is not a love-song, even though Mr Lamech is singing for
his wives. It is a murder-song. His great-great-grandfather
Cain at least had remorse when he killed his brother Abel.
Lamech speaks insultingly about the grace of God which is
truly 'seventy-sevenfold' powerful. Obviously, his two Mrs
Lamech sit down and listen to it. But Lamech – and all the
Lamech civilizations – is under the judgment of God which
mysteriously contains that note of 'not so!'.

Then comes the story of the Flood. The introduction to this great story is in four concise statements, and in this brief preface the message of the Flood is already given.

The Lord saw that the wickedness of man was great in the earth, and that every imagination of the thoughts of his heart was only evil continually. And the Lord was sorry that he had made man on the earth (a 'foolish' thing to say), and it grieved him to his heart (a 'weak' thing to say). So the Lord said, 'I will blot out ... '. But Noah found favour in the eyes of the Lord (6.5-8).

The world has become a world of 'continuous evil'. God decides to 'blot out' all living creatures. But in the last short sentence hope and salvation ring out as the two words 'Not so!' did for Cain. The central message of the story of the Flood is not located in the destruction of all living creatures, but in the fact that 'Noah found favour in the eyes of the Lord'. Its theological emphasis is not placed on destruction but on salvation. While it describes a comprehensive 'blotting out', we are impressed not by destruction but by the promise and the future given to Noah, his children and all the animals that floated in the ark!

Now we come to the story of the Tower of Babel (11.1-9). People built an impressive pyramidal temple (' ... a half-cosmical, half-religious symbolism: the 7 storeys represented the 7 planetary deities as mediators between heaven and earth; the ascent of the tower was a meritorious approach to the gods; and the summit was regarded as the entrance to heaven')[3] in the fertile Tigris-Euphrates basin.

'Come, let us make bricks and burn them thoroughly ... ' Let's do a careful job, mobilizing all technology available, particularly the advanced technology of using 'fire', since through this building programme we are going to place ourselves at the centre of the universe and we are going to be the symbol of human aspirations and ability. So, let's not just have a flat city made up of post offices, railway stations, hotels, restaurants, bakeries, launderettes. Let's have a city

with a distinctive character, a religious city which provides us
with the entrance to heaven. We do not feel quite free and
powerful unless we know how to 'handle' heaven. One way to
'handle' heaven is to have an easy technological approach to
heaven. When we have done this, we can get hold of heaven
because we have put a 'handle' on it! What is the use of such a
great investment if we cannot achieve this!? And let's make a
name, a religious name that refers to our deep self-identity. A
tower is a symbol of the centre of history. From the centre *we*
say 'Where are you?' to God and fellow men. So we now
speak the centre-of-history language! We have put a 'handle'
on history.

The story ends abruptly with 'Babel'. 'The Lord confused
the language of all the earth.'

Both the judgment and the grace of God upon the severe
outbreaks of sin progress from the Fall to the Tower. The
primeval history is not placed under either judgment or grace.
It is placed under *both*! The theological situation of primeval
history is not an easy one to 'handle'. Now this primeval
history under the judgment and grace of God stops abruptly
with the story of the Tower of Babel. At the end of the story, it
does not say, ' ... the Lord God approved Oxford English and
appointed it to become a unifier in the chaotic linguistic
situation'. We do not find the note of 'garments of skins', 'Not
so!' and 'Noah found favour in the eyes of the Lord' here. 'Is
God's grace finally exhausted?'[4]

The description of the primeval history is short. Yet with
amazing sharpness and eternal relevance it mirrors the history
of nations in the past and present. Primeval history is rightly
called 'history' in the sense that it makes the history we
experience today 'theologically historical' by inviting us to
hear the 'Where are you?' of God in our own history. The
story of primeval history comes out of the historical experience
of the covenant life of Israel. In the biblical world, the
historicity of a person is not of itself self-sufficient and replete
with meaning. To say that the man called Ahaz existed in
history does not of itself have theological value. But because

Ahaz was addressed by God's historical 'Where are you?' – because his historicity is met by God's historicity – his historicity has become full of meaning and definitely important. When the historicity of God's 'Where are you?' is intermingled with the historicity of a person, the person becomes 'historical', that is, 'theologically historical'.

I wish to take you to South East Asia now. It is there that I have tried to hear God's historical words of action, 'Where are you?' Our life in South East Asia is going through crisis, as is life anywhere in the world today. Our traditional experience with time, family, language and education is radically disrupted and confused. At these critical points we have lost our *šālôm*. We feel injured.

Time was traditionally experienced as being as unlimited as a loving mother's milk is unlimited to her baby. Time was generously given. It was not sold as pork chops are sold. There was no business engagement about time. Time was cyclical, that is to say, calm and level-headed. It was basically pastoral and agricultural. It moved in comforting rhythm with the ploughing in the paddy-fields. It was communal. Indeed, the essence of our experience of time can be said to be a sense of continuity of communal fellowship. We never experienced time in isolation. Apart from community no time existed. We floated communally in the ark of Noah. There was only one shared time on our ark.

Now, this has been changed without any consultation with us! Time is now to be understood in terms of business achievement. Time is now located in the export-import companies, motor-cycle manufacturers, stores and shops, instead of being in the paddy-field, under the coconut trees and in the temple yards. Time is now violently grasped. It was once public community property. It is now private business property. Once it was shared, now it is monopolized. Time does not heal us now. Time wounds us. *great* ☹

Family! Yes. 'Belonging to the family, belonging to the clan' was the primary value in our life. Family is the source of security, fellowship, encouragement, happiness, education

and spirituality. Family was sacred. The family has now been
invaded by the foreign value called 'money'. Cash relationship
is replacing personal relationship in our society today. *We
want* to have money. More money indeed. There are so many
attractive things around us! By the power of money we can get
them! We belong to money now. We do not know how to
control this powerful monster called cash. We do not know
how to hold it with a ring in its nozzle as we do our
waterbuffaloes. It is a new monster attacking our basic value.
It makes some of us like a Cain or a Lamech.

We have enjoyed speaking our own tongues. Ours are beautiful languages. We are proud of them. We can express ourselves
confidently and poetically. But as Sri Lanka became a 'tea
island' for the sake of the tea-drinking British masters, we
were forced to learn the languages of our masters. We were
not involved in empire-tower-building. We were victims. Yet
our languages began to be confused. The empires brought
their gifts, but with them came confusion and injury. After
Japan was defeated in 1945 we attained independence.
Independence meant freedom. Yet now, in 1975, we are not
free in our own countries. Our speech is brutally controlled.
Our own leaders are all out to cut our tongues off with a sharp
knife. The Singapore Prime Minister Mr Lee Kuan Yew has
been outspoken in expressing 'South East Asian gratitude' to
the United States for their massive intervention in Vietnam,
since it 'gave time' to the other South East Asian countries to
concentrate their own economic development. But it is
obvious to all today that the 'precious time' was wasted and
misused! In all the countries the rich became richer, the poor
became poorer. The living standard of people has been
worsened. It has indeed been a 'blessed' time for exploitation
and repression! Everything we say is examined lest it threaten
the national security! We cannot say what must be said!

Traditionally, education was not an accumulation of
English letters after our names. Education was personality-
formation. Today education is a tool to get a good job. Good
education brings more money. Isn't this a 'Lamech

education'? What is education for? What are academic degrees for? What is education? We are confused!

These are the historical situations we experience today. We want to know the mind of God – God's 'Where are you?' – in these concrete situations. These crises came about because some humans have 'handled' history brutally. Man can 'handle' history only through deceptions and the perpetration of injury to his neighbours. Perhaps this is the main characteristic of the 'outside-the-garden civilization'. Some of us 'handle' history on a greater scale than others. But none of us is free from this temptation of 'handling' history. We are all mutually 'handling' each other. In this sense we are fallen. We are active. We are powerful. Yet, we are fallen.

I am not suggesting that South East Asia can be understood theologically only in the light of primeval history. Primeval history is only one portion of the rich biblical tradition, and I am taking this section only as one example. Here as in other places God is portrayed as the one who does not 'handle' history. He rules history. He does not 'handle' history. He comes to history in which sin accelerates. His grace correspondingly increases. Does not this point to God's 'non-handling' rule over history? But how about the Tower of Babel? 'Is God's grace finally exhausted?'

The abrupt end of the story of the Tower of Babel is a moment of explosive theological silence. It is a moment in which both the end of the story of primeval history *and* the beginning of the new history – the call of Abraham – are prepared (12.1-3). Primeval history from the Fall to the Tower ends in Abraham, who begins the blessing-history: ' ... and by you all the families of the earth shall bless themselves.' He is not called for his own benefit. His call is an 'international' call. When he is called on behalf of the nations, all the nations are called. Abraham is a theological person in whom God's 'Where are you?' rings out to the nations. He became, therefore, the father of the multitudes (17.5).

Abraham historicizes and personifies God's 'Where are you?' This is done in a strongly 'historical' way – through the

promise of land and posterity. What a concrete, empirical and
down-to-earth promise it is! Everyone wants land and
posterity. Malaysians want them. Filippinos want them.
Japanese want them. They represent tangible continuity of
blessing. But this tangible blessing comes to Abraham only
when he believes God against all human possibilities.
Abraham believes in God 'without a handle' over God, land
and posterity. Abraham is intensely historical because his life
has been addressed by God's 'foolish' and 'weak' words. Did
not Sarah laugh? What does the name 'Isaac' mean? From
Mesopotamia to Canaan he journeys. His journey by itself is
neither spectacular nor historically significant. Mao Tse-
Tung's 1934-1936 Long March of nearly 6000 miles is far
more dramatic and eventful. Abraham's 'long march' is
meaningful only in its theological message. Through this
man's life bound up with the promise of the land and
posterity, God's 'Where are you?' is to reach the nations. As
long as Abraham means the historical continuity of God's
'Where are you?', he continues to be a theologically
meaningful model in our interpretation of history. 'Europe is
Egypt. America is the Promised Land.' (!) Has God's 'Where
are you?' reached the nations through the migrations from
Europe to America?

Tracing God's 'Where are you?' in our historical
experiences of human life, individual and collective, and
seeing God's attitude ('respecting', 'non-handle') towards our
history is the work of the theological mind, indeed, of the
crucified mind.

(b) The hands neither open nor closed – Buddha, Lenin and
    Jesus

I hope you have a mobile Christian mind which can move
from one historical context to another at an instant's notice. I
think such a quick shift is possible, since we believe that God's
'Where are you?' (God in search of man) gives unity and

continuity to the various contexts of culture, history and experience.

In Kyoto, Japan, there is an impressive image of Buddha made of copper in the Hakuho period (between the latter half of the seventh century and the eighth century). This image, a national treasure, has been speaking to the Japanese people through the centuries in their times of tranquillity and confusion. It is its hands which have a striking message. There is a web, like that of a duck, between the fingers. The webbed fingers derive from the religious and philosophical tradition of India. They are one of the thirty-two distinctive physical signs of the Buddha. Japanese people have understood this web to represent the intention of the Buddha to scoop all into salvation. No one will fall into the realm of darkness from between his saving fingers! The hands, well proportioned, attractive, merciful and confident, are a moving symbolism of divine salvation. They do not reject people. They are seeking people. They are inviting people. I thank God for this image. It expresses the depth and width of human need for salvation by the hands of good-will and mercy.

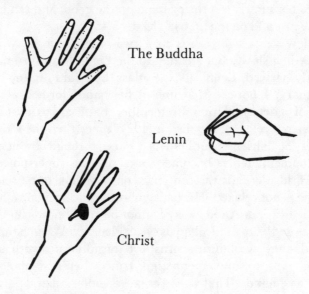

The Buddha

Lenin

Christ

The hands of the image are softly open in beautiful curves. They are purposefully open. There is no feeling of pain or agony. The image is strikingly 'religious', since religion must indicate a profound sense of 'indiscrimination' rooted in mercy. Mercy which chooses its object cannot really become a foundation for religious experience. When 'indiscriminate' mercy – the intense mercy – meets man, he surrenders and his religious life begins. True, theology cannot live without making distinctions ('sheep and goats', Matt. 25.32; 'law and gospel', Rom. 3.21; 'salvation and condemnation', John 3.17; and so on). But theology must be acquainted with the indiscriminate dimension of the mercy of God too. Sometimes theological arguments which endlessly elaborate distinctions, demarcations and discriminations (for instance, elaborate arguments for denominational*ism*!) are too 'wise' and too 'strong' to communicate the 'foolish' and 'weak' mercy of God. I maintain that mercy which has never reached the depth of indiscriminateness is not merciful enough to save sinful man. ' ... God had consigned all men to disobedience, that he may have mercy upon all' (Rom. 11.32); ' ... for he makes his sun rise on the evil and on the good, and sends rain on the just and on the unjust' (Matt. 5.45).

A few years ago, I was in a two-mile queue in Moscow proceeding slowly but steadily to the Lenin Mausoleum. As I silently viewed Lenin in the glass box laid in the inner sanctuary, I noticed that one of his hands formed a fist, a symbol of determination. I remember that I said to myself that he was not relaxed. He died in 1924. Since then the Union of Soviet Socialist Republics has gone through tremendous development. It has become one of the two super-powers of the world. Perhaps the time has come for him to be relaxed. But he is not relaxed. His fist symbolizes ideological rightness and dedication. An ideology cannot be really powerful unless it is 'closed'. Open ideology is weak ideology. When hands are closed, they symbolize a grasp of the ultimate truth and a strong will to implement that truth. Lenin cannot have Buddha's hands. That would create a confusion and paralysis at the centre of his message. Buddha addresses himself 'indiscriminately' to sinful man. Lenin addresses himself 'discriminately' to the proletariat against the bourgeoisie.

I do not quite understand, but I sense that the truth cannot be simply 'open'. When truth defines itself, it makes a movement toward 'closing', as human life inevitably moves towards death which is said to be the moment of truth. Truth demarcates its reality against other possibilities. The truth carries within itself the power of exclusion and 'closing'. The Hebrew word for truth, *ēmeth* (used 132 times in the Old Testament), is etymologically derived from the word that means 'to be firm, stand firm, be reliable, unchangeable'. For my children I am the father. This truth 'stands firm', since it excludes the possibility of other men naming themselves as the father of my children.

On the side wall of Newman College Chapel in Melbourne there is a bronze sculpture of Jesus on the cross. I used to look at it every day, since it was located on our short path to the grocery store. The nails brutally pierced the palms of the hands of Jesus. The weight of his body was painfully focused on these nails. He is in agony. He is gasping. He is neither like the Japanese Buddha with webbed hands, attractive and merciful, nor like Lenin with his confident ideological fist. Jesus looks defenceless. He is beaten. He is defeated. 'He was crucified in weakness … ' (II Cor. 13.4). His hands are neither open nor closed. Perhaps he wanted either to open them all the way or to close them all the way. I don't know. 'My Father, if it be possible, let this cup pass from me; nevertheless, not as I will, but as thou wilt' (Matt. 26.39) – this is what we hear. Did the nails actually pierce through the palms of his hands? I don't know. I am speaking the language of symbolism. I 'saw' that his hands are neither open nor closed. If his hands are closed tight, theology can become ideology. I am not suggesting that ideology is something inherently evil. There are good ideologies and bad ideologies. And none of us is free from ideologies. What concerns me here at this moment is that there is a distinction between

theology and ideology. Theology is 'neither open nor closed'.
'And blessed is he who takes no offence at me' (Matt. 11.6). If
his hands were open – very much open with symbolic webs –
then theology can get rid of its quality of being a 'stumbling
block'.

As I pondered the bronze figure of the crucified Jesus, I
began to see gradually that the saving truth which the gospel
speaks is spoken through hands which are neither open nor
closed, the crucified hands. God is not simply *ēmeth*. He is *hesed*
(grace, loving-kindness) too (Exod. 34.5-7). He is *ēmeth* in his
hesed. Is this not a theologically striking intersection (cross)?
He carried his cross with hands neither open nor closed!

I do not know how to relate systematically these crucified
hands to the webbed hands of the Buddha and to the clamped
hands of Lenin. All forms of hands – the hands of welcome,
the hands of rejection, the hands of hope, the hands of despair,
the hands of determination, the hands of love, the hands of
understanding ... must be related to the crucified hands
because the crucified hands are painfully neither open nor
closed. The crucified hands are the hands of ultimate love and
respect for our history. They are the hands of divine invitation.
The mind that contemplates the crucified hands, neither open
nor closed, is the crucified mind. The crucified mind is
perceptive about the varieties of forms of hands and their
relationship to the crucified hands.

In this strange form of painful hands, the crucified mind
perceives its explosive spiritual energy. In its 'weakness' and
'foolishness' it becomes far more resourceful than all the
'lunch-boxes' put together. The crucified mind guides the
positive energy of the 'lunch-box' in the direction of the
crucified Lord. The hands of Jesus are 'Where-are-you?
hands' of God.

The crucified mind confesses with Paul: 'As surely as God is
faithful, our word to you has not been Yes and No. For the
Son of God, Jesus Christ, whom we preached among you,
Silvanus and Timothy and I, was not Yes and No; but in him
it is always Yes. For all the promises of God find their Yes in

him' (II Cor. 1.19,20). This Yes is the Yes that comes from the crucified Lord. It is not an ordinary Yes. It is an extraordinary Yes we hear as we watch the crucified hands, the hands neither open nor closed.

4   The Face with Eyebrows Shaved Off

The King of Thailand shaved his head and eyebrows in 1956
when he entered the royal monastery.

Self-denial is the religious activity.

'I bear on my body the marks of Jesus.'

The form of religion is not simply that of 'a tower with its
top in the heavens'. It is also a form of Abraham sacrificing Isaac.

I wish to take you to an incident which happened to me in
Singapore several years ago. Singapore is almost on the
equator. When it rains, the air becomes immediately steamy
as the humidity rises. On one such rainy afternoon I was
driving with a Sri Lanka Buddhist monk in my small car. The
streets were, as usual, jammed with traffic and the fumes were
unbearable. The monk, reading from a huge church poster
'Crusade for Christ', turned and whispered to me: 'Your
Christ must be desperate. He needs his people to crusade for
him. Why do you Christians campaign for Christ?
Campaigning is a political exercise, and certainly not a
religious activity.' After a few minutes of silence he continued;
'Self-denial is the religious activity. Why do you cheapen and
humiliate your saviour?'

He was clad in an orange robe. His rubber sandals were
worn (Singapore $4.00 a pair when they are new), and over
his shoulder hung one empty cloth bag. The sight of Buddhist
monks has become familiar to me over the years. But this
whisper in the steamy Singapore afternoon made the monk
sitting next to me someone unfamiliar. He seemed suddenly
filled with a mysterious meaning and message for me. I took
an astonished look at the monk. I saw in him the
personification of the Buddhist history of the self-denial mind.
The imitation of the Buddha! This man lives in the Singapore

of today – a city of mushrooming shopping centres, of non-stop orchestration of advertisements; committed to the hysterical conviction that what we have is more decisive than what we are, and that what we eat is more important than what our body needs; and in which the word self-denial was long ago discarded as an idiotic virtue – he lives as a sign of self-denial in the broad day light of that city.

He does not own a Datsun 1100. He does not own a house. He does not have a wife. He does not have children. He does not have insurance. He does not have a pension arrangement. He does not depend upon a mission board. He does not own trousers or wear shoes. His robe does not have even one button. His clothes are button-free. He does not carry even one key. He lives in a key-free world. His is a living 'open city'. He is a no-defence-line person. And, mind you, he shaves off his hair and eyebrows! (The King of Thailand, His Majesty Bhumibol Adulyadej, shaved his head and eyebrows in 1956 when he entered the royal monastery.) He has denied himself the beauty of subtle expressive movements of the eyebrows! Does not Helena Rubinstein's multi-million dollar industry (and Max Factor, Dorothy Gray, Revlon, Elizabeth Arden, Shiseido ...) suggest that eyebrows should receive a great emphasis? Cannot our civilization today be symbolically called an over-emphasis-on-eyebrow civilization? He is against the spirit of our civilization. He is a self-denier. He is a renouncer in the midst of the commercial, industrial, science-technological and First National City Bank world.

> With downcast eyes, not loitering,
> With guarded senses, warded thoughts,
> With mind that festers not, nor burns,
> Fare lonely as rhinoceros.

> Shed thou householders' finery,
> As coral tree its leaves in fall:
> And going forth in yellow clad,
> Fare lonely as rhinoceros.

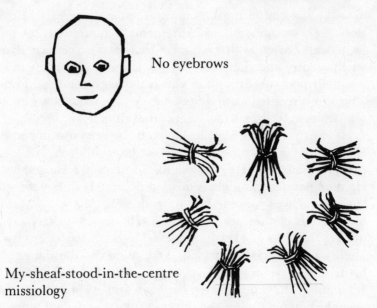

No eyebrows

My-sheaf-stood-in-the-centre
missiology

'Self-denial is the religious activity', my friend said. I do not
think that the varied and long history of human religious
experience can all be neatly subsumed under the concept of
self-denial. Human religiosity is a subject which defies a
simplistic approach. Religiosity is a cultural expression of
man's experience with the holy. Such experience is ever-living,
and it manifests itself in all directions. The religious situation
is thus ambiguous and uncontrollable. 'Self-denial is the
religious activity' – this is not a definition of religion. It is a
confession of a religious man about religion. I find this
confession moving. It has made me look at religious people in
a more concrete and appreciative way. The practice of self-
denial is surely one of the fundamental religious experiences of
the great historic religions. I am tempted to say that the
presence or absence of acts of self-denial must be a
fundamental criterion for the life inspired by religious
teachings. Neither organizations, nor authority-systems, nor
worship customs, nor ponderous dogmatic writings, nor a

right conception about divinity, nor cultic family and community life constitute the central religious experience. All these 'religious thoughts and acts' become genuinely religious experience *only* when they are grounded in the mind in self-denial. 'If any man would come after me, let him deny himself ... ' The religious mind is a self-denial mind. A religious act is a renouncing act (a symbolic no-eyebrow face!). It was the act of renunciation of the 29-year-old Siddharta Gotama that inspired millions to follow the path towards the highest good of *Nirvana* which he showed. For the Buddhists the story of renunciation is inseparable from the story of enlightenment. This confession of the monk has been meaningful for my theological life. 'If any man would come after me, let him deny himself and (shave his eyebrows) and follow me' is then a strong religious call!

You may not like this emphatic focus on self-denial. I know that such a suggestion is out of fashion today. You are afraid that self-denial will lead us to a pessimistic monastic mentality and a defeatist negativist psychology. I think that is quite possible. But it has not so led us in the profound messages of the living traditions of the great religions such as Hinduism, Buddhism, Confucianism, Judaism, Christianity and Islam. Authentic self-denial taught in these traditions is charged with explosive spiritual energy.

The central idea to which all the branches of Buddhism give deep spiritual and intellectual devotion is that of the inseparable unity of *wisdom* and *mercy*. The Buddhist wisdom is not a 'philosophy' as the West would define it. It is a 'path'. Walking on this path must be accompanied by doing the acts of mercy. They are inseparable. Self-denial roots itself in this unity of wisdom and mercy. This unity necessarily expresses itself as an act of self-denial. The motivation to self-denial is found at the very centre of the Buddhist way of life. In short, if one is devoted to wisdom and mercy, then one's life will one way or another concretely indicate the dimension of self-denial. Joachim Wach writes:

I should be inclined to think that acts of devotion and service to one's fellow-men are universally valid practical expressions of religious experience. It is the exception rather than the rule that in our modern Western civilization, worship of one's God and care for one's brother could become separated and one played against the other. If we can be proud at having left behind the cruder practices of an extreme asceticism, there is less reason for rejoicing that so many of us moderns have at the same time, because we see no motivation for it, abandoned all and every act of self-denial.[5]

The separation of wisdom ('worship of one's God') and mercy ('care for one's brother') is an exception in Western civilization. These two have gone together as a whole. But a strange difference occurs between the Buddhist tradition and that of Western civilization. In the former the unity between wisdom and mercy motivated the ideal of self-denial, while in the latter, people have been unable to see any motivation for self-denial and hence have 'abandoned all and every act of self-denial'. Western civilization is not a direct embodiment of Christian values and faith. Yet it is undeniable that Western civilization has been historically much closer to the teaching of Christianity than any other civilization. Christ took self-denial seriously. The whole gospel radiated from the self-denial of Jesus Christ. 'For the Son of man also came not to be served but to serve, and to give his life as a ransom for many' (Mark 10.45). In this passage, as among many others, self-denial is found rooted in the unity of wisdom and mercy. At what points did Western civilization muffle the original Christian inspiration of the religious and social value of self-denial? Meanwhile Gandhi is called 'Great Soul' by Tagore because of his personal act of self-denial. One of the most vivid religious images in Asia is still the picture of Gandhi in a simple loin-cloth, barefoot, walking on the village paths. To renounce oneself for the sake of others or for the sake of the truth is the inner secret of the glory of religious man.

Electricity becomes a living reality when it runs a train. Religion becomes a living reality when it creates self-denial in the life and mind of man.

If a religious man invites another to come to embrace his religion, he must establish the truthfulness of his belief and his self-identity by no less an act than that of self-denial. In the remote Indian villages men accept the family planning message from men who have themselves gone through sterilization by vasectomy. The scar of the operation authenticates his message. 'I bear on my body the marks (*stigma* – brand stamped on slaves) of Jesus!' (Gal. 6.17). This *stigma* is the centre of Paul's self-identity and it is this that authenticated Paul's message. 'Paul, a slave of Jesus Christ ... ' (Rom. 1.1). The mark of self-denial is the fundamental qualification for being an evangelist. Religious commitment can be communicated only through the sign of *stigma*. The suffix *-ism* in English language does as much harm as good. When this suffix makes words such as Hinduism, Buddhism, Judaism, and so on, it gives a strong impression that these 'religious systems' are neatly packaged one from the other and are objects of rational discourse. The historical reality of religious life has been far more imaginative and creative than any *-ism* can contain. Perhaps Hindu-*stigma* or Buddha-*stigma* would catch the life reality of religious phenomena more aptly than Hindu-*ism* and Buddhi-*ism*. *Ism* can be communicated without the sign of *stigma*. Religion cannot be communicated without it. Religion communicated without the sign of *stigma* is in truth no longer religion. It is a 'religion-business'. I have often been puzzled by missionaries persuading their Asian friends to change their faith from Buddha to Jesus Christ (Mind you, this is a 'big asking'. In Thailand this means that a person has to renounce his self-identity and often the means to support his family!). They themselves are not ready to change one iota of their rigid theological position or denominational security and self-identity. People do not see the *stigma* of Jesus Christ there.

In the Central Celebes, the tropical mountainous land of

the Traja people (thirteen hours by bus from the nearest
airport city of Makassar), one finds Amsterdam Christianity
complete with the Heidelberg Catechism and the Belgic
Confession. (Do you know the Belgic Confession?) Luther's
Larger Catechism is supreme in the land of the Bataks in
North Sumatra. The Heidelberg Catechism and Luther's
Larger Catechism are no doubt great monuments in the
history of Christian theology and ministry. I was not sorry to
see them there, but I am puzzled why and how they could
have remained intact, in their original forms, in lands of such
tremendous spiritual and cultural wealth. Wasn't there any
need to adjust them or at least to change expressions in a
fundamental way? In truth, there ought to be a Traja-berg
Catechism instead of the Heidelberg Catechism and a Batak
Catechism instead of Luther's Catechism.

The insight that comes from a life of self-denial will create
refreshing excitement in our theological and ministerial
engagements. This is because self-denial points to 'the form of
Christ' (Gal. 4.19). Amsterdam Christianity in the Celebes
does not reflect 'the form of Christ'. It definitely lacks the
insight of self-denial. Theology which is not rooted in the
aspiration and frustration of the local people is an a-historical
(docetic) theology. It gives people an impression that the
Christian faith is neither rooted in, nor concerned about,
history.

When I was teaching a Thailand Theological Seminary in
Chieng Mai, Thailand, I had a student whom I might have
called 'slow' I asked him one day to prepare a two-page digest
on one of the articles from *The Interpreter's Dictionary of the Bible*.
It took him two days. He worked hard. In his hands I saw an
English-Thai dictionary firmly grasped. Red-eyed, he
struggled with his assignment through breathless heat (and
mosquitoes). What he produced, however, was so confused
that I marked a few words upon it and gave it up. Later I went
out on an evangelistic tour with him. This time the position
was completely reversed. He became the professor and I
became the red-eyed student. He instructed me where to find

things, how to take a shower from the well, what to do about mosquitoes. He was thoroughly at home with his people. He became so creative. He was even able to crack 'theological jokes'! I gave a theological meditation. He somehow managed to translate it into the dialect and the people heard much more than what I said. With the *Dictionary* he could not make the grade, but with his own people, he made a beautiful passing grade, *cum laude*. How free he was! – as free as a bird flying in the blue sky over the tops of the tall coconut trees. He loved his people. He was concerned about them. He visited them. At two o'clock in the night he jumped out of his bed to take a sick man to hospital. He paid the taxi fare out of his own pocket. He did not ask any mission board or church office to reimburse the expense. But his school grades were miserably low. Should school adjust to him or he to school (with a traditional 'Western curriculum')? His own people saw the *stigma* of Jesus in him. Our theological education must be adjusted to the *stigma* of Jesus, and not the other way around.

What is academic excellence in theology? One who can read the Old Testament in Hebrew is more academically proficient than one who can read it only in Indonesian. Or if someone is readily able to benefit from *The Interpreter's Dictionary of the Bible* without much difficulty, he is academically more excellent than the Thai student I described. I think this makes sense. Academic excellence refers to the ability to use particular skills and tools. But academic excellence must not be appreciated by itself in isolation. Its value must be brought out in terms of excellence in serving man. 'To serve man' – this is the fundamental context in which academic excellence must be appreciated, since it is here that academic excellence can demonstrate its human value. Academic excellence is a part of human excellence. Human excellence is hidden in 'the form of Christ'. Academic excellence must receive the *stigma* of Jesus Christ.

The *stigma* of Jesus Christ! May I continue on this theme for a few more paragraphs? Let me quote one section from Gandhi's *An Autobiography, The Story of My Experiments with*

Truth. Here is an account of Gandhi's encounter with Mr
Coates;

> He saw, round my neck, the *Vaishanava* necklace of Tulasi-
> beads. He thought it to be superstition and was pained by
> it. 'This superstition does not become you. Come, let me
> break the necklace.' 'No, you will not. It is a sacred gift
> from my mother'. 'But do you believe in it?' 'I do not know
> its mysterious significance. I do not think I should come to
> harm if I did not wear it. But I cannot, without sufficient
> reason, give up a necklace that she put round my neck out
> of love and in the conviction that it would be conducive to
> my welfare. When, with the passage of time, it wears away
> and breaks of its own accord, I shall have no desire to get a
> new one. But this necklace cannot be broken.' Mr Coates
> could not appreciate my argument, as he had no regard for
> my religion. He was looking forward to delivering me from
> the abyss of ignorance.[6]

I think Mr Coates is sincere. He is, unlike most of us,
serious about his faith in Jesus Christ. His theological position
is clear and strong. I appreciate Mr Coates who is not
'lukewarm' (Rev. 3.16). ' ... Come, let me break the necklace'
– is not this a strong and straightforward proposal? Yes. He is
resourceful. He carries his 'high-protein lunch-box'. But his
resourcefulness is not trained and guided by the crucified
mind. In this sense, his resourcefulness is a dangerous one. It
is like a powerful train without an engineer. He wants to put
his hands upon the necklace 'she put round my neck out of
love'. He is resourceful, but he is superficial. He does not go
one step beyond the discussion of 'superstition'. He does not
see the shining presence of the love of Gandhi's mother in the
form of the necklace. He is more concerned about magical
effects of the necklace than is Gandhi. Gandhi sees love and
Mr Coates sees superstition in the necklace!

Mr Coates stands in the tradition of the dream of Joseph:
'Behold, we were binding sheaves in the field, and lo, my sheaf
arose and stood upright; and behold, your sheaves gathered

round it, and bowed down to my sheaf' (Gen. 37.7). What a non-self-denial dream! What a self-aggrandizement dream! I do not see any possibility of building edifying and healthy missiology upon this dream. The 'my sheaf arose and stood upright' missiology was unequivocally enunciated by Pope Nicholas V to Henry the Navigator. This papal bull (1454) exercised a far-reaching negative colonial and religious impact upon the lives of millions of Asians in the centuries to come:

> Our joy is immense to know that our dear son, Henry, Prince of Portugal, following the footsteps of his father of illustrious memory, King John, inspired with a zeal for souls like an intrepid soldier of Christ, has carried into the most distant and unknown countries the name of God and has brought into the Catholic fold the perfidious enemies of God and of Christ, such as the Saracens and the Infidels. ... We, after careful deliberation, and having considered that we have by our apostolic letters conceded to King Affonso, the right, total and absolute, to invade, conquer and subject all the countries which are under the rule of the enemies of Christ, Saracen or Pagan.[7]

Pope Nicholas lived in a world that did not have the telegram, television, jet planes and paperback books. His world-outlook was naturally severely limited. Yet, it was tragic that his *apostolic* letter was no more than a straight expansionist application of the Joseph's-dream theology. His apostolic letter (of 'after careful deliberation') does not show forth 'the form of Christ'. It was indeed powerfully written and has exerted powerful influence. But it 'cheapened and humiliated our Saviour'. The Joseph-Nicholas-Mr Coates line of theology does not represent the apostolic line of the gospel of Jesus Christ. Apostolic theology must be a 'stigmatized' theology. It must be rooted in apostolic self-denial. ' ... we have become, and are now, as the refuse of the world, the offscouring of all things' (I Cor. 4.13).

Missionaries should flow ever more freely from and to all six continents in a spirit of humble service.[8]

The 'spirit of humble service' means the deep awareness that missionaries are 'the refuse of the world, the off-scouring of all things', and the life-style that points to this humility before God.

I wish to say that self-denial means 'to live with the *stigma* of Jesus Christ'. This is the theological structure and meaning of self-denial. This is the 'christological' character of self-denial. Do we live with this sign? Is our life continuously made uneasy and insecure (!) because of the *stigma* we bear? 'Out of the depths I cry to thee, O Lord' (Ps. 130.1). My friend the monk walks in Singapore with the *stigma* of the Buddha. He bears the sign of the Buddha. His self-denial is 'buddhalogical'. His orange robes and his empty bag point to the ideal of the monastic life, the value of homelessness that Buddha taught.

He was obviously deeply puzzled by the campaigning behaviour of Christians. In many parts of Asia we come across a 'Crusade for Christ'. In Hong Kong, Singapore, Taiwan, Thailand and Korea crusades come in waves. Asians know intuitively that the holy man Jesus Christ cannot be the man of religious crusade. Strangely Asia knows Jesus Christ as the self-denier. The holy man is the self-denier. Am I just suggesting that the wording 'Crusade for Christ' should be dropped? What I am really aiming at here is to place such campaign psychology of Christians under the light of the New Testament theology of the *stigma* of Jesus Christ. What does the *stigma* of Jesus Christ mean in our evangelism? Every crusade event in Asia accentuates the tragic discrepancy between the 'theology of the *stigma* of Christ' and the 'theology of the crusade for Christ'. In this discrepancy I see an equally serious sign of discrepancy between Asian spirituality and that of the Christian West. In rejecting the 'theology of the crusade for Christ' intuitively and emotionally, the Asians are indicating their genuine openness to the alternative, the theology of the *stigma* of Christ. Asians know what self-denial and *stigma* mean through their own history and experience. The biblical salvation history moves with the sign of the *stigma* of Christ, not with the religious campaign.

Am I against campaigning at all? Am I saying that all campaigning is futile? No. I am simply saying that within the context of the apostolic church ('the refuse of the world, the offscouring of all things'), the crusading mind must be baptized by the crucified mind so that human resourcefulness will become resourceful 'in the sight of God'. The church remains apostolic as long as the crucified mind stands in its heart and cries to the crucified Lord. 'For I decided to know nothing among you except Jesus Christ and him crucified' (I Cor. 2.2). The *stigma* of Jesus Christ must fundamentally overshadow any campaign for Christ. Then the 'campaign for Christ', the crucified, the 'most stigmatized', will become a 'stigmatized campaign' which is already *no longer a campaign or crusade* in an ordinary sense. 'If any man would come after me, let him deny himself and take up his cross and follow me' (Matt. 16.24).

We live today between two sayings of Paul: 'Let every person be subject to the governing authorities. For there is no authority except from God, and those that exist have been instituted by God' (Rom. 13.1), *and* 'We impart a secret and hidden wisdom of God, which God decreed before the ages for our glorification. None of the rulers of this age understood this; for if they had, they would not have crucified the Lord of glory'. (I Cor. 2.7,8). We must subject ourselves to the governing authorities, but none of the rulers of this age understood the mystery of the crucified Lord. This is the 'difficult time' in which we live our historical life. And let us not forget what the history of the church tells us. Often the church lived comfortably on the side of 'the governing authorities' who do not understand the glory of the crucified Lord. As long as we live in this tension, we cannot simply retreat into quietism. We must act and speak out for the truth in whose light we have found the meaning of our life. But our action and our speaking out must be guided by the inspiration of the one who is crucified for us. I am suggesting something more than some adjustments to be made in our method of evangelism. I am stating the need for recovery and renewal of the *apostolic character of the church*. The apostolic mind is primarily and fundamentally the crucified mind, not the crusading mind.

Early in my work in Thailand, my neatly established system of Christianity was challenged. The focus of the issue was 'non-Christian spirituality', which virtually no theological textbooks talked about when I was a theological student. My system, which I thought to be an enlightened and broad-minded one, told me that somehow an authentic spirituality can be born and nurtured only by the power of the gospel of Jesus Christ. This scheme made me regard the spirituality of Thai Buddhists as either undernourished or misguided. It was not the subject of the difference of history and doctrine between Christianity and Buddhism that caught my attention. That has not given me 'spiritual' trouble. But I was shaken by the reality of Buddhist spirituality. I came to know the people who call themselves Buddhists 'with fragrance of the Buddha'. They live a life of piety, humility and dedication to the ideal given by the Buddha. Above all, their poverty and the freedom they enjoy in being poor impressed me. I cannot define spirituality. It is a kind of fragrance that comes from the depth of personality. How is Buddhism capable of producing men of such spiritual beauty? I had thought it was a monopoly of Christians. Yet, I have known people of fragrance (II. Cor. 2.14) not only among Christians but also among the Buddhists, Hindus and Moslems. Often I was bothered by a contrast between the security-minded and budget-minded Protestant missionaries and the orange-robed Buddhist monks in Thailand. In their spirituality the monks appeared closer to the image of the stigma of Christ than the Christian missionaries! Is such a thing possible!?

Someone might say that it is true that Buddhism is capable of such a noble spirituality, but that the basis of Buddhist spirituality is a wrong one. In short, it looks inspiring, but in truth it is a crooked and rotten spirituality, since it is not rooted in the name of Jesus Christ. I have heard this said to me on countless occasions. This is a powerful 'solution'! This solution will give us sense of security! Isn't it assuring to know that after all only Christian spirituality is the true spirituality? Such self-admiration theology – how deeply is this theology responsible for the crippling spiritual parochialism within the church! – has no place in the gospel of Jesus Christ. 'Love is patient and kind; love is not jealous or boastful' (I Cor. 13.4). 'Let him who boasts, boast of the Lord' (I Cor. 1.31). Boast of the *crucified* Lord! How can one boast of the crucified Lord with the crusading mind and with the crusading 'solution'? The apostolic mind is not a self-admiration mind. It is better to be merciful in the name of the Buddha than to be cruel in the name of Christ. It is better to become a neighbour with a Samaritan theology (presumably a wrong theology in the view of the Jews) than to desert the beaten victim with Jewish theology (presumably a right theology in the view of the Jews). 'Go and do likewise!' (Luke 10.37). If one is merciful in the name of Christ, if one becomes a neighbour to the needy, one will certainly not make such derogatory comments on the spirituality of the men of other living faith.

'The wind blows where it wills, and you hear the sound of it, but you do not know whence it comes or whither it goes; so it is with every one who is born of the Spirit' (John 3.8). The breath of self-denial is the wind of spirituality. Spirituality is fragrant when it contains self-denial. Christian spirituality is beautiful and edifying when it lives with the stigma of Christ's self-denial. 'Blessed are the poor in spirit, for theirs is the kingdom of heaven' (Matt. 5.3).

I want to go back to the monk. You remember that I concurred with his focusing on self-denial. I said that religion is alive when it creates the man of self-denial. I am even tempted to say that 'Greater religion has no man than this, that a man lay down his life for his friends'. The religious life lives by the secret of sacrifice and self-denial.

Karl Barth, in the chapter of his *Church Dogmatics* called

'Religion as Unbelief', has this to say:

> ... in religion he ventures to grasp at God. Because it is a
> grasping, religion is the contradiction of revelation, the
> concentrated expression of human unbelief, i.e., an attitude
> and activity which is directly opposed to faith.

Religion is grasping! 'The form of religion' contradicts 'the
form of Christ'. 'The form of religion' is 'a tower with its top in
the heavens'.

In the desperate few years leading up to 1945, 'the hundred
million children of the divine emperor' defended the 'Sacred
Land of the Rising Sun'. Everyone in Tokyo recited: 'This is
the palace of the emperor, the palace of the emperor, the
palace of the emperor.' The American B29s saturated Tokyo
with devastating fire bombs and Tokyo became a wilderness.
In August, as the nuclear bombs fell over Hiroshima and
Nagasaki, the Satan of absolute State Shintoism also fell like
lightning from heaven. On 1 January 1946 the emperor issued
the Imperial Rescript Denying His Divinity. Eighty years of
the murderous Shinto paganism was officially rejected. Living
through these times, I know what Barth is speaking about.
Religion is grasping!

Yet, this is not the whole picture of the religious experience
of mankind. Religious reality is ambiguous. It contains both
demonic and angelic possibilities. The great historic religions
have through the centuries resolutely stood for 'non-grasping'.
They taught repeatedly against human greed. They insisted
on the building up of the human community through love and
mutual respect. They have, in fact, created countless people
who have led the non-grasping life. Such people did so out of
their faith in the ultimate truth and out of love for their
neighbours. Gandhi was dedicated to the ideal of *aparigraha*
(non-possession) taught by the *Bhagavad Gita*.

'The form of religion' is not simply that of 'a tower with its
top in the heavens'. It is also a form of Abraham sacrificing
Isaac. The outright negative estimation of the living religious
traditions of the world must have come from a failure to

appreciate the reality of self-denial in these religious lives. One must look at the religious reality with one's eyebrows shaven. Christian theology and ministry have consistently looked upon the religious life of man only negatively. The theology of the *stigma* of Christ requires us to take a careful and humble look at the lives of religious men.

5 'Hear, O ... '

The centrality of self-denial heard in

(*a*) 'Hear, O Israel ...'
(*b*) 'Hear, O Christians ...'
(*c*) 'Hear, O Muslims ...'
(*d*) 'Hear, O Hindus ...'
(*e*) 'Hear, O Buddhists ...'
(*f*) 'Hear, O Confucians ...'

What I am going to do in this section makes me feel like a country mouse (a near-sighted one!) trying to speak about the great elephant. But still I wish to venture to do it. I believe that the central messages of the great historic religions are very much with us in such a way that the history in which we live today is responding to them in profound and mysterious ways. To my mind this hidden dialogue between the historic spiritual messages and our history today points to the very enduring value of these time-honoured spiritual 'words' (*dharma*).

(*a*) The *shema* of Israel: a call to love the covenant God

Hear (*shema* in Hebrew), O Israel: The Lord our God is one Lord; and you shall love the Lord your God with all your heart, and with all your soul, and with all your might (Deut. 6.4).

This is an imperative language. Yet, it is far more than that. It is covenant-relationship language. There is a historic memory of 'I am the Lord your God, who brought you out of the land of Egypt, out of the house of bondage' (Exod. 20.2) behind the *shema*. In that sense it is a reminder of the salvation history experienced by Israel. 'God loved you with all his heart, and with all his soul, and with all his might' (' ... the

Lord brought us out of Egypt with a mighty hand and an
outstretched arm, with great terror, with signs and
wonders ... ', Deut. 26.8), therefore God wants you to
remember this *shema* and practise it for your own spiritual and
physical prosperity.

It is therefore quite impossible to understand the
commandments in Deuteronomy as 'law' in the theological
sense of the word, as though Deuteronomy were leading
Israel to earn salvation by a total obedience. Rather, all the
commandments are simply a grand explanation of the
command to love Jahweh and to cling to him alone (Deut.
VI.4f.). And this love is Israel's return of the divine love
bestowed upon her.[10]

This *shema*, this call to love the personal covenant God,
shapes the basic spirituality of the adherents of Judaism,
Christianity and Islam. Thus over one billion people today
come under the inspiration of this one passage, Deut. 6.4. I
locate the secret of the power of the *shema* in the historical
experience of the covenant people of God, in particular of
persons like Hosea who saw with deep human feeling where
the people stood in relation to the covenant-faithful God.[11]
The *shema* points to the suffering of the covenant God who
found himself with an unfaithful people. Apart from this
specific entanglement of two histories – the history of the
covenant-faithful God *and* the history of the people who do not
love 'the Lord your God' – the *shema* could not have displayed
its continuing historical forcefulness. As we listen to the *shema*,
as the call coming out of the entanglement of the two histories
(though indeed are one history), we are led to see the
dimension of the 'self-denial' of God! Here is 'a grand
explanation of the command to love Jahweh'. I wish to call
your attention to Hos. 11.7-9. I am doing this to remind
ourselves of the presence of the moving theological experience
which is behind the *shema*.

My people are bent on turning away from me, (in spite of

the shared historical and covental experience) So they are appointed to the yoke, and none shall remove it. How can I give you up, O Ephraim! How can I hand you over, O Israel! How can I make you like Adamah! How can I treat you like Zeboim!

When He acts in love, God demonstrates no less than His proper character as the holy God. Hence He suffers under the lovelessness of His people, whose covenant faithfulness is only like the morning dew which quickly dispels (6:4). In face of its sin He is overcome by a kind of helplessness.[12]

Helplessness of God! His hands are painfully neither open nor closed. He must give up Ephraim, but he cannot give up Ephraim! He is caught!

My heart recoils within me
(self-denial!),
my compassion grows warm and tender
(post self-denial compassion, compassion informed by self-denial)
I will not execute my fierce anger
(self-denial!),
I will not again destroy Ephraim
(decision rooted in God's self-denial),
for I am God and not man
(is this act of God's self-denial a pointer to the meaning of 'I am God and not man'?),
the Holy One in your midst,
(Is this act of God's self-denial a pointer to the meaning of the Holy One? Does this mean that God stands in our midst in self-denial? Is 'midst' the place of 'self-denial' theologically speaking? 'And with him they crucified two robbers, one on his right and one on his left'. (Mark 15.27).) and I will not come to destroy
(Salvation and the beginning of new history flow from God's holy self-denial!).

Is not this the secret of the power of the *shema*? It points to the living personality of God. *For a short moment* the inner emotion of this God is revealed in the most moving way – the way of God's helplessness and his self-denial! ' ... you shall love the Lord your God with all your heart, and with all your soul, and with all your might.'

(*b*) The Christian *shema*: a call to follow Jesus Christ

If any man would come after me, let him deny himself and take up his cross and follow me. For whoever would save his life will lose it, and whoever loses his life for my sake will find it (Matt. 16.24).

The Christian *shema* is a call to self-denial and to follow the one who denied himself! Self-denial receives its meaning from Jesus Christ, since the love of God is demonstrated through the crucified Jesus. 'But God shows his love for us in that while we were yet sinners Christ died for us (Rom. 5.8).

(*c*) The Islamic *shema*: a call to submission to God

The religious life which began in the early seventh century in the Arabian world with the Prophet Muhammad (570-632) is called Islam. The canon of the faith, the Qur'an, names this faith Islam, which means 'submission'. 'The true religion with God is Islam' (*Qur'an* iii, 'The House of Imran'). 'Today I have perfected your religion for you, and I have completed My blessing upon you, and I have approved Islam for your religion'. (*Qur'an* v, 'The Table').

The *Adhān* (the call to the divine service of Friday and the five daily *salāts* – prayers) contains the Islamic *shema*: 'Allah is most great. There is no god except Allah and Muhammad is the Apostle of God.' *Allah akbar* (Allah is most great) is the centre of the Islamic *shema*. He is the Unique One. He is the Alone. He has no associates whatsoever. 'In the Name of God, the Merciful, the Compassionate. Say: "He is God, One, God, the Everlasting Refuge, who has not begotten, and has not been begotten, and equal to Him is not any one" '. *Qur'an* cxii, 'Sincere Religion'). He is the Majesty beyond man's knowledge and understanding. He does not 'limit' himself. He has not 'bent down' to the people. He does not suffer. He is never 'helpless'.

What gives unity to all God's dealings is that He wills them all. He, as Willer, may be recognized from time to time by means of the descriptions given. But He does not essentially conform to any. The action of His will may be identified in this or that quality: His will of itself is inscrutable. One may not, therefore, say that God is necessarily loving, holy, righteous, clement, or relenting, in every and all relations.[13]

Islam is the meeting between God as such and man as such.[14]

The relationship between God and man is submission. Man is a slave (*abd*) to God. If you are 'submitted to God' (*muslim*), you must observe the law of God:

And slay not your children for fear of poverty; We will provide for you and them; surely the slaying of them is a grievous sin. And approach not fornication: surely it is an indecency, and evil as a way. And slay not the soul God has forbidden, except by right. Whosoever is slain unjustly, We have appointed to his next-of-kin authority; but let him not exceed in slaying; he shall be helped. And do not approach the property of the orphan save in the fairest manner, until he is of age. And fulfil the covenant; surely the covenant shall be questioned of. And fill up the measure when you measure, and weigh with the straight balance; that is better and fairer in the issue. And pursue not that thou hast no knowledge of; the hearing, the sight, the heart – all of those shall be questioned of. And walk not in the earth exultantly; certainly thou wilt never tear the earth open, nor attain the mountains in height. All of that – the wickedness of it is hateful in the sight of thy Lord (*Qur'an* xvii, 'The Night Journey').

Do these things as a *muslim* and because you are *muslim*. 'Walk not in the earth exultantly!' You are not that big! Only *Allah akbar!*, 'submitted to God', is the Islamic *shema* to self-denial.

(d) The Hindu *shema*: a call to desireless action

Let me quote few passages from the *Bhagavadgita*, the book that has exercised far-reaching spiritual influence throughout the centuries and has blossomed in our century in the mind of Gandhi at the time of the national crisis.

> He who has no ill will to any being, who is friendly and compassionate, free from egoism and self-sense, even-minded in pain and pleasure and patient.
> He who has no expectation is pure, skilful in action, unconcerned, and untroubled, who has given up all initiative (in action), he, My devotee, is dear to Me.[15]

I understand that the call to freedom from 'egoism and self-sense' and more precisely the call to renunciation of the expectation of obtaining the fruits of one's actions is one of the central messages of the Hindu world. Man is free when he is free from the 'expectation' of the fruits of his action. He who can perform desireless action is 'pure'. I am lecturing at a university. Am I not thinking of the salary I shall receive? I am greasing a car at a garage. Am I not thinking of the income I make out of this labour? I am taking care of my own children. Am I not thinking that they will some day assist me when I retire? I am working hard in a company. Am I not thinking of promotion? I am believing in God. Am I not thinking that I might go to paradise some day? I love my neighbour. Am I not thinking that the neighbour will love me and help me in return? I am giving my life for a noble cause. Am I not thinking that I will somehow get it back because what I have done is of great merit?

How in the world can I do anything without thinking of the fruits of my action? How can I even understand 'I do' apart from 'I gain'? Are not 'I do' and 'I gain' inseparably related in

my mind and in my soul? How can I renounce the fruits of my
actions? ' ... better than meditation is the renunciation of the
fruits of action; on renunciation (follows) immediately peace'
(xii, v.12). The *Bhagavadgita* says that only when one gives up
the idea of the fruits of one's action does one attain 'peace'. 'I
do my duty. That's all. No more!'

> Does he thank the servant because he did what was
> commanded? So you also, when you have done all that is
> commanded you, say, 'We are unworthy servants; we have
> only done what was our duty' (Luke 17.9,10).

Honest work must bring honest gain. But when 'I do' is
always 'I do *because* I gain', such 'I do' will threaten our
civilization. I cannot but agree with Gandhi that freedom of 'I
do' from 'I gain' is the cornerstone for the non-violent world.
This message has a strong relevance, since our world today is
too consistently and decisively that of 'I do because I gain'.

The Hindu *shema* is the call to 'desireless action' (*nis-
kamakarma*). Desireful action is a self-aggrandizement that will
destroy the peace in the human community. Desire-less is
'pure' since it is self-less. Out of self-less actions comes a
possibility of an *ahimsa* (non-violent) world. Is there anything
that mankind needs more today than the reality of *ahimsa*?
Self-denial is denial of violence.

(*e*) The Buddhist *shema*: a call for the extinction of cravings

Here is the Buddhist *shema*:

> What now, O monks, is the noble truth of Suffering?
> Birth is suffering, old age is suffering, death is suffering,
> sorrow, lamentation, pain, grief and despair are suffering.
> But what, O monks, is the noble truth of the Origin of
> suffering? It is that Craving, which gives rise to fresh rebirth
> and, bound up with pleasure and lust, now here now there,
> finds ever fresh delight.
> But what, O monks, is the noble truth of the Extinction of

suffering? It is the complete fading away and extinction of this craving, its forsaking and giving up, liberation and detachment from it.

But what, O monks, is the noble truth of the path leading to the extinction of suffering? It is the noble Eightfold path, namely: right understanding, right thought, right speech, right bodily action, right livelihood, right effort, right mindfulness and right concentration.

These are the Four Noble Truths which Gautama Buddha, the Enlightened One, preached in Deer Park outside Benares and thus set the wheel of the law into motion. The tradition says that prior to this proclamation Gautama spent six years (from his twenty-ninth to his thirty-fifth year) in ascetic meditation. One of the most touching sculptures I have seen is the famished ascetic Gautama in the intense meditation posture placed in the inner yard of the Marble Temple in Bangkok. The image is a striking symbolism of self-denial.

The Four Noble Truths progress from the truth of suffering to the origin of suffering, then to extinction of suffering and finally to the path leading to the extinction of suffering. It concentrates itself on the question of human suffering. There are no gods (or God) who suffer. Only man suffers. And he makes himself suffer. Thoughts on gods and God are not profitable, since they hinder man from looking at himself, and it is he who makes himself suffer. When man speaks about his own existence, he is, in truth, speaking about his suffering: 'Birth is suffering'. To begin to be is to begin to suffer. Isn't this an extreme thing to say? Isn't this destructively pessimistic?

The relationship between the truth about suffering and the origin of suffering was commented upon by the perceptive Thai Buddhist monk Buddhadasa Bhikkhu:

But birth is *not* suffering, ageing is *not* suffering, death is *not* suffering in a case where there is no grasping at 'my' birth, 'my' aging, 'my' death. At the moment, we are grasping, regarding birth, aging, pain and death as 'mine'. If we don't grasp, they are not suffering; they are only bodily changes. The body changes thus, and we call it birth; the body changes thus, and we call it ageing; the body changes thus, and we call it death. But we fail to see it as just bodily changes. We see it as actual birth, and what is more, we call it 'my' birth, 'my' ageing, 'my' death. This is a multiple delusion because 'I' is a delusion to start with; so seeing a bodily change as 'my' birth or 'my' ageing is yet a further delusion. We fail to see that these are simply bodily changes. Now just as soon as we do see these as just bodily changes, birth, ageing, and death disappear, and 'I' disappears at the same time. There is no longer any 'I'; and this condition is not suffering.'[16]

I suffer because someone ate *my* pizza. Eliminate 'I' and 'my' from this sentence. Then you are in tranquility, *nirvana*. It is greed (*tanha*) that creates suffering (*dukkha*). My 'I' is a big 'I'. This is my greedy relationship with my 'I'. Big 'I' wants to have 'my' big pizza. When someone eats 'my' big pizza, I 'deeply' and 'enormously' suffer.

The ideal man in Buddhism is the non-grasping man, the free-from-'I' man, the man who denies himself in a thorough-going way. There is a popular Thai poem among the Thai country people:

Beauty is to be found in the dead body.
Goodness is to be found in non-grasping.
A monk is to be found in one's conscience.
Nirvana is to be found in death before death.

Destroy your *tanha-dukkha* syndrome! When you do this you are saved. Your greedy relationship with yourself is the source of your suffering. 'If any man would come after the Buddha, let him eliminate his "I". ... '

The concept of the *Bodhisattva* (a 'being'-*sattva*, destined for 'enlightenment', buddhahood – *bodhi*) is one of the outstanding features of the great history of Mahayana Buddhist religious life. *Bodhisattva* are beings who have made a vow many existences ago and have accumulated an immense amount of merit. So far as they are concerned, then, they are free from the snares and entanglements of this world. If they so wish, they can reach the final release, the *nirvana*. But their concern is no longer about their own salvation but the salvation of all sentient beings. They postpone their entrance into *nirvana* and work for the salvation of all by identifying themselves completely with the needs of the people. They offer themselves for the welfare and eternal bliss of all beings. The Buddha is looked upon as the supreme of the *Bodhisattvas*.

For infinite past kalpas,
The World-honoured One has practised
All manner of virtues with effort
To bring benefits to us human beings,
Heavenly beings, and dragon kings,
Universally to all living beings.
He abandoned all things hard to abandon,
His treasures, wife, and child,
His country and his palace.
Unsparing of his person as of his possessions,
He gave all, his head, eyes, and brain,
To people as alms.
Keeping the buddhas' precepts of purity,
He never did any harm,
Even at the cost of his life.
He never became angry,
Even though beaten with sword and staff,
Or though cursed and abused.
He never became tired,
In spite of long exertion (ch. 1, *The Lotus Sutra of Innumerable Meanings*).

The Buddha, the Self-Denier, the Altruist, the Total-Giver, is the source of the perennial inspiration of the Mahayana tradition. The goodness of the Buddha is found in his perfect non-grasping. 'If any man would come after the Buddha, let him become a *bodhisattva* who gives himself for the benefit of others ... '

(f) The Confucian *shema*: a call to the highest virtue, *Jen*

The Analects of Confucius (552-479 BC) can be read in two
days. It is amazing that such a small ancient book of
fragmentary sayings has been able to exercise such an
enormous spiritual influence upon the Chinese people and
whoever came into contact with the civilization of China. The
centre of the proclamation of Confucius is *jen*. In the Analects,
as many as 58 chapters touch upon the discussion on *jen*, and
the word *jen* itself appears 105 times in all. Yet all these *jen*-
related sayings refer to the ways of attaining *jen*, and
Confucius is silent about *jen* itself or the essence of *jen*. He
points to *jen* from various directions. But he does not analyse
its essence. He does not possess it in his hands. Instead, he lets
jen grasp him (as the *daimon* spoke to Socrates). The *jen* that he
does not speak of directly – the *jen* that took hold of him –
impresses the readers of the Analects with mysterious force.

> Chung-kung asked about perfect virtue (*jen* – love,
> benevolence, charity, humanity, virtue, compassion, mercy,
> kind-heartedness, graciousness, generosity, sympathy,
> consideration, goodness, goodwill, tenderness). The Master
> said, 'It is, when you go abroad, to behave to every one as if
> you were receiving a great guest; to employ the people as if
> you were assisting at a great sacrifice; not to do to others as
> you would not wish done to yourself; to have no murmuring
> against you in the country, and none in the family' (Book
> xii, ch.2).

One of the main pointers to *jen* is, as is suggested in
the above quotation, the principle of reciprocity (*shu*,
consideration for others, forgiveness, reciprocity). Here is the
Confucian *shema*:

> Tsze-kung asked, saying, 'Is there one word which may
> serve as a rule of practice for all one's life?' The Master
> said, 'Is not reciprocity (*shu*) such a word? What you do not

want done to yourself, do not do to others.' (Book xv, ch.24).

Remember *shu*. Practise *shu*. Is it difficult to practise? Yes. 'Tsze-kung said, "What I do not wish men to do to me, I also wish not to do to men." The Master said, "Tsze, you have not attained to that". ' (Book v, ch.12). Yet this is the way to *jen*. In the practice of *shu* man comes to *jen*. He will then become a truly educated and virtuous man. He lives with *jen*. He lives in the light of *jen*. He is a new man. He is a new creation. 'The Master said, "If the will be set on virtue (*jen*), there will be no practice of wickedness".' (Book iv, ch.4).

The secret of the power of the Confucian *shema* is not simply located in the wise, truthful and penetrating words of Confucius. Again it is rather in the image of the sage who put the whole of his personality – 'with all your heart, and with all your soul, and with all your might' – to the practice of *shu*. He lived in the hope of the appearance of the kingdom of *jen*, in individual as well as national life. He lived in the promise of *jen*. 'The Master said, "Is virtue (*jen*) a thing remote? I wish to be virtuous, and lo! virtue (*jen*) is at hand" ' (Book vii, ch.29). 'There were four things from which the Master was entirely free. He had no foregone conclusions, no arbitrary predeterminations, no obstinacy, and no egoism' (Book ix, ch.4).

'If any man would come after Confucius, let him practise the principle of reciprocity ...' Believing in the promise of the kingdom of *jen* and sincerely doing one's utmost to usher such a kingdom into the world through the way of *shu* is the Confucian way of self-denial.

I would characterize the six *shemas* as follows:

(*a*) The *shema* of Israel

The covenant God seeks man who is unfaithful in the covenant relationship. In this seeking, God himself goes through self-denial.

(*b*) The Christian *shema*

Jesus Christ humbled and emptied himself. He was crucified 'for many'. 'Deny yourself. Take up your cross and follow me.'

(*c*) The Islamic *shema*

Allah akbar. Therefore man is not *akbar*. Man is a servant. He is submitted (*muslim*) to the law of the Merciful and Compassionate.

(*d*) The Hindu *shema*

Desire in action must be rooted out (denied). *Ahimsa* comes to us through desireless actions.

(*e*) The Buddhist *shema*

Destroy (deny) *tanha*, then *dukkha* will cease. Imitate the self-giving and self-denying *bodhisattvas*!

(*f*) The Confucian *shema*

Observe the sacred duty of reciprocity (deny ego-centricity). The kingdom of *jen* is at hand.

6 People of the *Shemas* and Jesus Christ

'Whither shall I go from thy Spirit?'

The *shemas* speak extreme language.

' ... but afterwards he repented and went.'

The Buddhists say neither 'Jesus is Lord' nor 'Jesus be cursed'.

'And Jesus looking upon him loved him.'

There is today a profound sense of spiritual uneasiness among us. We are educated. We are modern. We are scientific. We have had considerable experience in political and economic organization. We are schooled in the histories of nations and are aware of the historical whereabouts of our own nations. Yet, for all our enlightened understanding, we find our sense of identity disintegrating. Our existence is being threatened. Our communication is breaking down. Our sense of value is crippled. We feel ourselves to be living in a time of *spiritual* crisis for mankind. I do not think there is among us anyone who can offer a satisfying explanation of why we are where we are today. We sense that somehow we are the very source of tragedy to ourselves. We are aware that it takes human spirit to bring forth human tragedy and equally that it takes human spirit to bring forth human glory. Our spirit is confronted by two awesome possibilities: human tragedy and human glory.

I call heaven and earth to witness against you this day, that I have set before you life and death, blessing and curse; therefore choose life, that you and your descendants may live, loving the Lord your God, obeying his voice, and cleaving to him; for that means life to you and length of days, that you may dwell in the land which the Lord swore to your fathers, to Abraham, to Isaac, and to Jacob, to give them (Deut. 30.19,20).

. Our spirit is not breathing in a historical vacuum. Wherever we are today upon this planet we come under the powerful influence of Western civilization. It is sometimes called scientific-technological civilization or simply modernization. Our everyday experience confirms that this latest civilization is the most forceful and most universal civilization that has ever appeared on the horizon of the history of mankind.

Western civilization is a strong spiritual movement. It has been often pointed out that Western civilization has fostered the world-view called secularism. Secularism is defined as 'anti-spiritual'. An antonym of 'secular' is thought to be 'spiritual'. But secularism is one form of spiritual orientation. It is a world-view in which human spiritual energy is directed toward 'this world' (*saecularis* meaning 'worldly', 'temporal'). Man is inescapably spiritual. It is the spirit of man that appreciates spiritual value. It is again the spirit of man that rejects spiritual value. Since it is the spirit of man that does these things, all *human* values carry inevitably the dimension of spiritual value. 'God is Spirit' (John 4.24) means 'man is spirit'. 'Whither shall I go from the Spirit? Or whither shall I flee from thy presence? If I ascend to heaven, thou art there! If I make my bed in Sheol, thou art there! ... ' (Ps. 139.7,8).

The Manifesto of the Communist Party (January 1848) by Marx and Engels is not simply a discourse on economic analysis. It is an outburst of human spirit against the spirit of social exploitation. It is in that sense a manifesto of human spiritual frustration and aspiration. Mao Tse-Tung, who stands in the tradition of *The Manifesto*, is much more a story-teller than an economic theory-teller. His story language comes straight into the spirit of the Chinese mass. Let me just quote one such story:

> To whom should the fruits of victory in the War of Resistance belong? It is very obvious. Take a peach tree for example. When the tree yields peaches they are the fruits of victory. Who is entitled to pick the peaches? Ask who planted and watered the tree. Chiang Kai-shek squatting

on the mountain did not carry a single bucket of water, and yet he is now stretching out his arm from afar to pick the peaches. 'I, Chiang Kai-shek, own these peaches,' he says, 'I am the landlord, you are my serfs and I won't allow you to pick any.' We have refuted him in the press. We say, 'You never carried any water, so you have no right to pick the peaches. We the people of the Liberated Areas watered the tree day in day out and have the most right to gather the fruit.'[17]

Here the great civil conflict between the Kuomintang and the Communist Party is brought into sharp focus by a simple story which speaks to the spiritual sentiment of the mass of the Chinese people. Mao spoke in his own way the message 'thou shalt not steal'. 'Thou shalt not steal' is a revolutionary as well as a spiritual message.

The *apartheid* policy of the South African régime is a 'spiritual' movement. That is to say, it comes from a human spirit which is misdirected. If it were not a movement of the misdirected spirit, it would have been much easier to correct it. Among the critical comments made by the Australian Council of Churches upon 'The Aborigines and Torres Strait Islanders Affairs Act of 1965' of the State of Queensland (the Act is still the basis of current practice in the State) one finds such comments as:

On Part I, Section 31: Since Aborigines under the 'Act' require permission to withdraw money from their accounts, the Department can ensure that a large total balance is left in the banking system it operates. It invests this in long-term high-interest loans and after paying bank interest makes a sizeable profit ($21,000.00 in 1969/70). This is the same system all banks use with one basic difference – you can withdraw your money from the bank whenever you wish. What is the money from this Fund spent on? Part was spent on buying Comalco shares, and some on a training school (trade) at Cherbourg reserve – both were widely publicized as proof of the generosity of the government to

the Aborigines. None of the press releases mentioned that
this generosity was paid for with the Aborigines' money.

Such an operation comes from greed-spirituality. In that
sense, it is a destructive 'spiritual' movement. If it were not
rooted in the greed-spirituality, it would be readily rectified.

The *shemas* are, to my mind, of critical importance as we try
to understand and live through the present time of turbulent
human spirituality. We are living at the point of transition
from tradition to modernization. In this transition we are
witnessing the work of massive misdirected spirituality, the
unclean spirit. The *schemas* are against greed-spirituality.
They are against stealing and cheating.

The *shemas* originated in the historical experience of human
spirituality. What they stand for is readily grasped against the
background of the experience of morality and the conscience
of mankind. The *shemas* speak to us and speak for us. They
point to the refreshing possibility of restoring personal and
communal integrity. The rejection of the value that the *shemas*
are trying to point out for us must be one of the most
fundamental reasons for the tragic world situation today. We
can ignore the messages of the *shemas*. But if we do so,
somehow we will injure ourselves. I do not claim to know why
it is this way. It must be a mystery that grasps us. Japan, in
her mad drive to increase the Gross National Product in the
past twenty years, has ignored and silenced the voice of the
shemas in her relationship with the nations in South East Asia,
and is now coming under the severe judgment of the peoples in
that region. The Australians suffer in their spiritual life
because of their unfair treatment of the aborigines. Man
cannot ignore these historic *shemas* without incurring serious
injury upon himself.

The *shemas* speak 'extreme' language. 'Love your God with
seventy per cent of your heart' is quite enough! On the
contrary, the *shema* demands a complete 'extreme' devotion to
God. ' ... with all your heart, and with all your soul, and with
all your might'. 'Deny yourself and *take up your cross* and follow

me' is an extreme thing to say. A hard saying indeed! That
man is essentially *abd* is also an extreme message. So are the
suggestions to separate 'I do' from 'I gain', the elimination of
tanha and a complete *reciprocity*. This extreme quality in the
shemas is strangely not destructive but creative, not deceptive
but truthful. Language becomes extreme when it tries to speak
against the spirit of self-aggrandizement. Each *shema* presents
self-restraint, self-control, self-denial as a historically more
meaningful and hopeful spiritual attitude for mankind than
the attitude of greed and self-aggrandizement. They are
extreme, yet they are fascinating. It looks as though they are
all gone and have disappeared, yet they are very much with
us. They sound like baby-talk in the world of astronomical
expenditure on armaments and of nuclear energy, yet they are
able to speak the language of ultimate human value, to which
even nuclear energy must be made submissive if man is to
remain human. In our day one way to characterize the voice of
the *shemas* is to quote this powerful and paradoxical statement
on the spiritual identity of an apostle:

> We are treated as impostors, and yet are true; as unknown,
> and yet well known; as dying, and behold we live; as
> punished, and yet not killed; as sorrowful, yet always
> rejoicing; as poor, yet making many rich; as having
> nothing, and yet possessing everything (II Cor. 6.8-10).

Jesus Christ stands *in the midst* (Hos. 11.9) of this world of
ours – the world of clean spirit and unclean spirit, the world
experiencing the violent transition from tradition to
modernization, the world in which man is inevitably
confronted by the great historic *shemas*. His hands are
painfully neither open nor closed.

> And as he was setting out on his journey, a man ran up and
> knelt before him, and asked him, 'Good teacher, what must
> I do to inherit eternal life?' And Jesus said to him, 'Why do
> you call me good? No one is good but God alone. You know
> the commandments: 'Do not kill, do not commit adultery,

Do not steal, Do not bear false witness, Do not defraud,
Honour your father and mother.' And he said to him,
'Teacher, all these I have observed from my youth.' And
Jesus looking upon him loved him, and said to him, 'You
lack one thing; go, sell what you have, and give to the poor,
and you will have treasure in heaven; and come, follow me.'
At that saying his countenance fell, and he went away
sorrowful; for he had great possessions (Mark 10.17-22.
See Matt. 19.16-22; Luke 18.18-23).

No man of the Buddhist *shema* or the Islamic *shema* 'ran up
and knelt before him' in the New Testament for obvious
geographical and chronological reasons. Here a man who
belonged to the tradition of the *shema* of Israel, to which Jesus
himself belonged, came to Jesus. His question was one that
comes out only from the mouth of a devout man of deep piety.
It is about 'inheriting eternal life'. He 'knelt before him' and
asked the question of his 'ultimate concern' (to use Tillich's
expression). Jesus answered him by quoting the
commandments. The man responded; 'Teacher, all these I
have observed from my youth.' Is this kneeling man arrogant?
Isn't it true that, as we watch such a drama at a comfortable
'theological' distance, our theology will immediately begin to
shout or murmur, 'How can anyone observe all these
commandments! In the sight of the holy God we are all
violators of the divine commandments!'

'*And Jesus looking upon him loved him.*' Jesus respected him and
appreciated him for his devotion and practice of the
commandments. He accepted him and his sincerity. Are we to
reject him? I believe there are a good number of people of the
shemas who can sincerely answer Jesus in the same manner.
The people of the Buddhist *shema* know similar
commandments *within their own historic context*. 'You know the
commandments; avoidance of destroying life, abstention from
taking what has not been given, abstention from unchastity,
abstention from lies, abstention from taking intoxicating
drinks.' 'Teacher, all these I have observed from my youth!'

'Think not that I have come to abolish the law and the prophets; I have come not to abolish them but to fulfil them' (Matt. 5.17). Jesus has come not to abolish 'avoidance of destroying life, abstention from taking what has not been given, abstention from unchastity, abstention from lies, abstention from taking intoxicating drinks', but to 'fulfil them'. He has not come to destroy the ideals of *ahimsa* and *jen* but to 'fulfil them'. The *shemas* stand against human greed. May I then say; 'And Jesus looking upon the one who leads greed-free life, the one who fights against the power of greed (Eph. 6.12), loved him.' In his love directed to him, 'he said to him, "You lack one thing ... " ' One thing! 'Go, sell what you have, and give to the poor, and you will have treasure in heaven.' Again, I believe there would be a fair number of people of the *shemas* throughout the centuries who could sincerely answer to this call; 'Teacher, I have done this!' Would not Jesus looking upon them have loved them! Yet, this is not the end of the story. There are four more words to come, ' ... and come, follow me'.

Who is this 'me'? Where is he today in the world among the *shemas*?

Is he alive today? Is he working in our history? Is he coming to us who belong to the various living *shema* traditions?

And behold, a lawyer stood up to put him to the test, saying, 'Teacher; what shall I do to inherit eternal life?' He said to him, 'What is written in the law? How do you read?' And he answered, 'You shall love the Lord your God with all your heart, and with all your soul, and with all your strength, and with all your mind; and your neighbour as yourself.' And he said to him, 'You have answered right; do this, and you will live.' (Luke 10.25-28).

The educated lawyer answered the question right. The *shema* of Israel resounded from his mouth. The lawyer was testing Jesus. But Jesus was sincere over the question which was posed to him and the answer given by the one who tested him. The lawyer spoke of the corner-stone of the spiritual tradition of the chosen people. Yet, this is not the end of the story. There are six more words to come:' ... do this, and you will live.'

Practise the shema! Then you will experience 'inheriting eternal life'. You can talk about eternal life. You can formulate the structure and the character of eternal life theologically. But 'you will live' comes only when you 'do this'! Knowing the commandments is important. To be able to answer correctly the question 'what is written in the law' is important. To know the need to 'Be merciful, even as your Father is merciful' (Luke 6.36) is an illumination to the spiritual life of man. But if he is not merciful even though he sees this illumination, then someone who is merciful even without knowing the merciful Father will stand closer to the mind and practice of the Father.

> What do you think? A man had two sons; and he went to the first and said, 'Son, go and work in the vineyard today.' And he answered, 'I will not'; but afterwards he repented and went. And he went to the second and said the same; and he answered, 'I go, sir,' but did not go. Which of the two did the will of his father? They said, 'The first.' Jesus said to them, 'Truly, I say to you, the tax collectors and the harlots go into the kingdom of God before you' (Matt. 21.28-31).

Why? It is because they 'repented and went'. Is not 'repented and went' fundamental in the preaching of Jesus? Does not the prodigal son in the parable 'repent and go'?

> But when he came to himself he said, 'How many of my father's hired servants have bread enough and to spare, but I perish here with hunger! I will arise and go to my father, and I will say to him, "Father, I have sinned against heaven and before you ... ' (Luke 15.17,18)

Does not Zacchaeus 'repent and go'?

> Behold, Lord, the half of my goods I give to the poor; and if

I have defrauded any one of anything, I restore it fourfold'
(Luke 19.8).

The people of the *shemas* – people who are dedicated to the
teaching of the Buddha, or of Muhammad, for example –
know what 'repented and went' mean in their own religious
devotional experience. They are well equipped to appreciate
the New Testament theology of 'repented and went'. They are
neither strangers nor uninitiated into this central theological
message of the Christian faith. They have their own
understanding of mercy and they practise mercy with their
spirituality. But they do not say that Jesus is the Lord. Even
though they practise mercy and they have experience of what
'repented and went' mean in their own context, since they do
not confess the name of Jesus Christ as the Lord, are they
separated from Jesus Christ?
   'Go, sell what you have, and give to the poor ... ' The man
'went away sorrowful; for he had great possessions'. *Went
away*! Does this mean that he does not belong to Jesus Christ?
Went away *sorrowful*! Sorrowful, not spiteful and arrogant. Is
he finished with Jesus Christ? 'How happy are those who
know what sorrow means, for they will be given courage and
comfort!' (Matt. 5.4: J.B. Phillips translation). Is then our
relationship with Jesus Christ so easily severed or broken? Is it
so fragile, like glassware? Is such a *going away sorrowful* the end
of the possibility of the community of grace in the name of
Jesus Christ who is called 'Emmanu-el (God with us)' (Matt.
1.23)? If our 'belonging to Jesus Christ' were so fragile, 'then
who can be saved?' (Mark 10.26). Isn't it a realistic thing to
say that sooner or later we come to the limit-line at which we
will 'go away sorrowful'? None of us can deny himself to the
extent that Jesus Christ (who said ' ... come and follow me')
denied himself! (Phil. 2.6-8) 'Then who can be saved? Jesus
looked at them and said, 'With men it is impossible, but not
with God; for all things are possible with God' (v.27). From
our viewpoint, 'went away sorrowful' immediately makes us
ask the question 'then who can be saved', but it is not so with

God! ' "Rabbi, who sinned, this man or his parents, that he was born blind?" Jesus answered, "It was not that this man sinned, or his parents, but that the works of God might be made manifest in him" ' (John 9.2,3). 'Went away sorrowful' and 'born blind' – what critical and despairing situations! – are looked upon differently from the viewpoint of God.

But, do they, the people of the Islamic *shema* or the Buddhist *shema*, and so on, belong to Jesus Christ? Do they? Indeed, they do practise mercy, and they do have spiritual experience of 'repented and went', but they have not confessed the name of Jesus Christ! Do they belong to Jesus Christ?

' ... no one speaking by the Spirit of God ever says "Jesus be cursed!" ' (I Cor. 12.3). The people of the *shemas* do not say 'Jesus be cursed!' I have not heard 'Jesus be cursed!' said by the people of the *shemas* during my work in South East Asia. I have often heard 'Christians be cursed!' Jesus Christ is respected. His name is holy. His name means goodness and blessing. The Buddhists respect Jesus Christ while the Christians do not show respect to the Buddha. This is an embarassing contrast which one sees in many parts of Asia. If Thai Buddhists hear an English speaking person swearing by the name of 'Jesus Christ' they are certainly deeply offended!

'No one can say "Jesus is Lord" except by the Holy Spirit' (I Cor. 12.3). Do the Buddhists say 'Jesus is Lord'? No. They say 'The Buddha is Lord' instead. But they do not say 'Jesus be cursed'! Then do they stand somewhere between 'Jesus be cursed' and 'Jesus is Lord'? In some nebulous middle-ground? I do not think so. I cannot define where they stand in relation to Jesus Christ. I know they do not say 'Jesus be cursed'. I know they do not say 'Jesus is Lord'. I believe Jesus Christ must know where they stand.

After the arrest of Jesus, Peter followed Jesus 'at a distance'. There he denied Jesus three times.

But Peter said, 'Man, I do not know what you are saying.' And immediately, while he was still speaking, the cock crowed. And the Lord turned and looked at Peter. And

Peter remembered the word of the Lord, how he had said to
him, 'Before the cock crows today, you will deny me three
times.' And he went out and wept bitterly (Luke 22.54-62).

Peter, the leader among the Twelve, denied Christ three
times. The number one disciple he was! Three times! Was his
relationship with Jesus destroyed and finished? Was it broken
up in hopeless pieces like a glass fallen on to the concrete
pavement? Does he, the rock (Matt. 16.18), still belong to
Jesus Christ after his emphatic denial? So far as he was
concerned, he was finished with Jesus. 'And the Lord turned
and looked at Peter.' Was it the look of condemnation,
rejection, disgust or forgiveness, communion, hope, life,
acceptance? How did Jesus Christ, the son of the God who is
faithful to the covenant, look at this man? The New
Testament does not tell us how and in what way Jesus looked
at him. But we see here the infinite beauty, amazing comfort
and powerful presence of the faithful God (Ezek. 37.1-14).
How can we see it? We see that Peter 'went out and wept
bitterly'.

The people of the other living faiths cannot betray Jesus as
Peter did. Betrayal is a possibility that can come only to those
who have been intimately committed. Peter's situation is an
extremely intense one. As I watch *this* Peter, the first among
the apostles, who has been restored by Jesus who 'turned and
looked at' him, I am guided to say that the relationship
between Jesus and the people of the *shemas* cannot be a
superficial and fragile one. Jesus Christ on his way to suffering
'turns and looks at' *all of us* since we all take part in this Peter
one way or another. Thinking about the relationship between
the Gospel of Christ and the people of the *shemas* must not be
disengaged from the Lord who is betrayed and on the way to
the cross. Only such a serious context of messianic suffering
provides illumination for such a serious subject. And no
theology can adequately describe and communicate the living
impact of the look of Jesus upon all of us.

Jesus Christ, in whom the Christian church believes, is the

head of the church and the head of the universe (Col. 1.15-20).
He is concerned not only with 'church history' but with
'human history'. Indeed there are not two histories: the
church and the human. He came to one history and died for
one total history. The *shemas* are not abstract messages. They
have originated in history and lived through history. The
shemas are experienced *shemas*. They are speaking to the minds
of the millions at this critical moment of human spiritual
crisis. The crucified one is drawing the peoples of the *shemas* to
himself in his way, the way of the mystery of self-denial of the
Son of God. 'To do his deed – strange is his deed! – and to
work his work – alien is his work!' (Isa. 28.21). Do we want to
know more? Yes, indeed! ... let us take time and look at Jesus
Christ who carries the *handleless* cross. What do you see *there*?

7 The Finger of God that does not Work Comprehensively

At Bethzatha Jesus healed only one man 'who had been ill for thirty-eight years'.

Invitation-theology versus answer-theology.

We walk with him even though our questions are unanswered.

Comprehensive theology produces straight-application theology.

My religion is better than yours! – We have had enough of the 'divine beauty contest'.

The unnecessary stumbling block and the genuine stumbling block.

'But if it is by the finger of God that I cast out demons, then the kingdom of God has come upon you' (Luke 11.20). The 'finger' here stands for the 'power' of God. The kingly rule of God is realized by the finger of God that casts out demons from our history. 'O faithless generation!' Jesus says (Mark 9.19). But he does not cast out the whole 'faithless generation'. 'He came to his own home, and his own people received him not' (John 1.11). But he did not condemn his own people as a whole (John 3.17). He, as the Word which was from the beginning, sustains and bears the faithless generation and his own people (John 1.1; Heb. 1.1-3). He does not engage in a scorched-land or a saturation bombing strategy. He does not change history 'comprehensively'. Jesus changes it 'fundamentally'. If history is changed fundamentally by Jesus Christ, the change should be obvious to everyone. Yet it is not self-evident. If he does change history comprehensively, his work would become obvious to us all. But that is not what he does. He directs himself to the *foundation* of our lives and gives us the *sign* for the reality of the kingly rule of God within our history. 'Lord, even the demons are subject to us in your name!' And he said to them, 'I saw Satan fall like lightning from heaven' (Luke 10.17,18). That 'the demons are subjected' to Jesus Christ points to the hidden *fundamental* change taking place within our history rather than obvious *comprehensive* change.

The gospel narratives tell us of healings performed by Jesus. But he did not perform healing comprehensively. At Bethzatha there was 'a multitude of invalids, blind, lame, paralysed'. Yet, Jesus healed only one man 'who had been ill for thirty-eight years' (John 5.2-9). Jesus said, 'Lazarus, come out!' (John 11.43). But he did not say 'all dead come out with Lazarus!' The Thai literary critic, Mr Kukrit Pramoy, once questioned why Jesus did not raise all the dead with Lazarus and why Lazarus later died his 'second' death. In his view this indicates that the claim of Christian salvation is after all not ultimate.

And he went about all Galilee, teaching in their synagogues and preaching the gospel of the kingdom and healing every disease and every infirmity among the people. So his fame spread throughout all Syria, and they brought him all the sick, those afflicted with various diseases and pains, demoniacs, epileptics, and paralytics, and he healed them (Matt. 4.23,24).

'Every disease and every infirmity!' Indeed, yet this does not mean that mankind is finally and 'comprehensively' freed from 'every disease and every infirmity'. They have been very much with us in the time of Jesus, before and afterwards. Healing both at Bethzatha and in the region of Galilee was a sign pointing to the finger of God. At Cana in Galilee, Jesus changed water into wine. 'This, the first of his sins, Jesus did at Cana in Galilee, and manifested his glory; and his disciples believed in him' (John 2.11).

The finger of God does not work comprehensively. But the finger of God which does not work comprehensively shakes the *foundation* of history. God does not grab history. God penetrates history. This makes us hopeful. This heals us. Such work of God in Jesus Christ demands faith from us: 'I believe, help my unbelief!' (Mark 9.24). The God who does not work comprehensively is the God who baffles us. 'Blessed is he who takes no offence at me' (Matt. 11.6). A 'comprehensive' God is an obvious God. The 'obvious' God is an idol. Idols we can tame, but we cannot domesticate the living God. Jesus Christ crucified is the furthermost point from idols. Why? He at this point becomes most intensely 'baffling', 'scandalous', 'mysterious', 'untamed', 'not obvious' and 'not comprehensive' to us.

The mind inspired by the idea of a comprehensive-obvious God produces passive answer-theology instead of lively invitation-theology. One of the unfortunate characteristics of the Christian mission in Asia has been the presentation of the gospel of Christ in terms of a slogan; 'Jesus is the Answer'. In my own Japanese language 'Jesus is the Answer' sounds extremely awkward, cheap and superficial. In my culture it would be understood as saying that Christianity works mechanically, therefore it has no significant spiritual dimension. But the real issue is not a cultural but a theological one.

Jesus Christ means a continuous *story*, not a *deus ex machina answer*. 'I am the way, and the truth, and the life; no one comes to the Father, but by me' (John 14.6). This passage is not saying that Jesus is the answer. Instead, Jesus is inviting us to come and walk with him. What is the use of knowing the way if one does not walk on it? No! Unless one walks on the way, one does not know the way. 'I am the way' means 'walk with me', the basic message throughout the biblical tradition. ' ... and the truth' means that as we walk with him we will see and experience his truth. And as we see and experience his truth we will be affected by his life. And being affected by his life we begin to say 'Abba, Father' (Gal. 4.6; Rom. 8.15). Jesus Christ is obviously neither like Mary Poppins who straightens out a messy children's room with a snap of her

fingers, nor like a Santa Claus who is carrying a bagful of
sweet answers for everyone. He is more interested in
establishing a relationship than in giving answers. He is the
God who is faithful to the Son of the Covenant (devoted
relationship). He stands firmly in this biblical tradition. 'For
it is better for them to find you and leave the question
unanswered than to find the answer without finding you'
(Augustine, *Confessions*, Book I, 6).

God called Moses at the critical moment of Israel's national
existence.

> 'And now, behold, the cry of the people of Israel has come
> to me, and I have seen the oppression with which the
> Egyptians oppress them. Come, I will send you to Pharaoh
> that you may bring forth my people, the sons of Israel, out
> of Egypt.' But Moses said to God, 'Who am I that I should
> go to Pharaoh, and bring the sons of Israel out of Egypt'?
> (Exod. 3.9,10).

B.D. Napier gives an exciting piece of exegesis;

> Who am I? asks Moses. Child of Israel-Egypt? Fugitive?
> Priest's son-in-law and Midianite shepherd? No, responds
> the Word. Your identity now is to be understood only in
> relation to Me. You are God-with-you.[18]

The answer God gave was a strange one: 'I will be with you.'
You are not going out on this mission other than on this basis.
'I will be with you' is the answer. Yes. But this answer is not
given in the style of Mary Poppins and Santa Claus. It is given
with the promise of the sign! It is given in terms of something
that will happen in the future. ' ... and this shall be the sign
for you, that I have sent you; when you have brought forth the
people out of Egypt, you shall serve God upon this mountain'
(Exod. 3.12). The sign that 'I have sent you' will be given in
the course of the work. Moses, whose identity is 'I will be with
you', is to walk with God and obey his voice, since as the giver
of this identity of Moses is living, so his identity must breathe
as a living organism towards the promise of God. 'You-are-

God-with-you' is future-oriented and faith-oriented. Such identity is a given-identity rooted in the grace of inviting God. The Exodus God is an invitation God rather than an answer-giving God.

Jeremiah goes through a similar experience in his soul.

'Before I formed you in the womb I knew you, and before you were born I consecrated you; I appointed you a prophet to the nations.' Then I said, 'Ah, Lord God! Behold, I do not know how to speak, for I am only a youth.' But the Lord said to me, 'Do not say, "I am only a youth"; for to all to whom I send you you shall go, and whatever I command you you shall speak. Be not afraid of them, for I am with you to deliver you, says the Lord. (Jer. 1.5-8).

Jeremiah felt a deep sense of insecurity and weakness at the moment of the call. He was appointed to be a prophet to Assyria, Babylonia, Egypt and Judah. He was to go and to speak only on the basis that 'I am with you to deliver you'. Throughout his ministry he felt the unbearable pain and strain of his office. In the extremity of his despair, Jeremiah addressed God in the language of profound personal grief and lament.

O Lord, thou hast deceived me, and I was deceived; thou art stronger than I, and thou hast prevailed. I am become a laughing-stock all the day; every one mocks me. For whenever I speak, I cry out, I shout, 'Violence and destruction!' For the word of the Lord has become for me a reproach and derision all day long. If I say, 'I will not mention him, or speak any more in his name' there is in my heart as it were a burning fire shut up in my bones, and I am weary with holding it in, and I cannot ... Cursed be the day on which I was born! ... Why did I come forth from the womb to see toil and sorrow, and spend my days in shame? (Jer. 20.7-9,14,18).

Let me quote Gerhard von Rad:

The word which we have rendered as 'deceived' in fact designates the act of enticing and seducing a young girl – 'you took advantage of my simplicity' (Rudolph). The prophet cannot really blame himself: his power and Jahweh's were too unequal. He admits that he attempted to escape from this intolerable service: but the word with which he was inspired was like fire in his breast. Therefore he had to continue to be a prophet. But what is to become of him as a result! His days are to end in shame (vs.18). And so finally – and this is the supreme consequence – Jeremiah curses the complete abandonment of his life (vs.14f). These last passages are soliloquies – the God whom the prophet addresses no longer answers him. ... It is still Jeremiah's secret how, in the face of growing scepticism about his own office, he was yet able to give an almost superhuman obedience to God, and, bearing the immense strains of his calling, was yet able to follow a road which led ultimately to abandonment. Never for a moment did it occur to him that this mediatorial suffering might have a meaning in the sight of God. Again, if God brought the life of the most faithful of his ambassadors into so terrible and utterly uncomprehended a night and there to all appearances allowed him to come to utter grief, this remains God's secret.[19]

God who promised Jeremiah 'I am with you to deliver you' is now silent. Jeremiah lives in faith without an answer. All he has is the promise 'I am with you to deliver you'. This promise itself now appears not to be in effect. Yet by giving 'an almost superhuman obedience to God' Jeremiah deepens the meaning of 'I am with you to deliver you'. He takes this promise with him deep into the secret of his soul. He agonizes. He laments. 'Why did I come forth from the womb to see toil and sorrow, and spend my days in shame?' *No answer.* Yet, he obeys God. Few people have had such a profound spiritual crisis and experience. Jeremiah reminds us of the last moment of the crucified Lord. 'My God, my God, why hast thou forsaken me?' (Matt. 27.46). Jesus cries to God even though he feels that God is forsaking him! 'He flees to God against God! O strong faith!' (Luther). Jeremiah and Jesus placed their trust in the forsaking God! Theirs is no longer the faith built upon God's obvious answer. They believed in God even though God did not answer! It is the profoundest possibility of faith in the covenant relationship. Here we do not see an answer-theology. We see instead a relationship-theology. In spite of all cruel odds, they believed in the invitation of God to walk with him, even though their agonizing questions were unanswered! An unnamed Canaanite woman shares in this type of spiritual trial. She cries to Jesus:

> 'Have mercy on me, O Lord, Son of David; my daughter is severely possessed by a demon.' But he did not answer her a word. ... But she came and knelt before him, saying, 'Lord, help me.' And he answered (and what an answer!), 'It is not fair to take the children's bread and throw it to the dogs.' (Then comes a marvellous confession of faith, stronger than many Apostles' Creeds!) 'Yes, Lord, yet even the dogs eat the crumbs that fall from their master's table.' Then Jesus answered her, 'O woman, great is your faith! ...' (Matt. 15.21-28).

The woman did not give up her hope even though 'he did not answer her a word'. She believed in Jesus, even though chilling brutal words were spoken to her. She did not stand on answer-theology. She stood in the living theology of relationship. She believed in Jesus who 'did not answer her a word'.

On numerous occasions I have heard the gospel of Jesus Christ being presented as a happy-ending religion. Giving one's Christian testimony. or witness is often meant to be telling people how Christian faith has given good health, good business and improved social position with better income. Jesus. can make you happy. He will solve your problems. 'Come unto him!' I am not saying that this is untrue. There must be a great number of people whose social position and

income has been bettered since they became Christians. But
the commitment to Jesus Christ may or may not improve
social position. The Christian faith has no basic relationship
with the improvement of social standing. Christian faith may
make you a happy man or make you say, 'Why did I come
forth from the womb to see toil and sorrow, and spend my
days in shame?' The gospel (good news) is anything but a
happy-ending religion. 'We know that in everything God
works for good with those who love him, who are called
according to his purpose' (Rom. 8.28). This passage has been
quoted often to support the happy-ending quality of Christian
faith. I understand this passage to destroy such an idea. An
exposition of the passage is given in II Cor. 11.23-29:

> Are they servants of Christ? I am a better one – I am talking
> like a madman – with far greater labours, far more
> imprisonments, with countless beatings, and often near
> death. Five times I have received at the hands of the Jews
> the forty lashes less one. Three times I have been beaten
> with rods; once I was stoned. Three times I have been
> shipwrecked; a night and a day I have been adrift at sea; on
> frequent journeys, in danger from rivers, danger from
> robbers, danger from my own people, danger from
> Gentiles, danger in the city, danger in the wilderness,
> danger at sea, danger from false brethren; in toil and
> hardship, through many a sleepless night, in hunger and
> thirst, often without food, in cold and exposure. And, apart
> from other things, there is the daily pressure upon me of my
> anxiety for all the churches. Who is weak, and I am not
> weak? Who is made to fall, and I am not indignant?

This is Paul who said 'in everything God works for good with
those who love him'. There is no increase of salary mentioned.
No business expansion spoken of. His calory intake has not
increased. His social standing has not improved. Paul's God is
not an 'obvious' God. He is not an idol. He is the living God.
Through Paul who was imprisoned, beaten, stoned,
shipwrecked, threatened by all kinds of people, hungry,

thirsty, cold and exposed, God touched the foundation of history, and he let Paul touch it too. Happy-ending religion is a cult of an obvious God who works comprehensively, whose finger moves only predictably. The living God of the Bible has been transformed into a predictable manager of happy-ending religion. He does not stand against man as the sovereign Lord. He now follows man's self-congratulatory view of religion! Most of the hymns sung in the Asian churches are dominated by the theology of Jesus Christ, the author of happy-ending religion. I count it to be a great misfortune that this God with the predictable finger was preached far more forcefully and universally in Asia than the God with the unpredictable finger. The God of the predictable finger (the answer-God) in truth looked too cheap to be true to the eyes of the Asians whose hearts are much more receptive to the message of the unpredictable finger of God (the invitation-God).

The theology of the 'comprehensive God' (God who works obviously and comprehensively and therefore became domesticated by man) expresses itself in straight-application theology. Straight-application theology is quick and efficient, like the many straight lines that were drawn efficiently by the colonial masters who divided countries in Africa. The Psalmist says, 'The fool says in his heart, "There is no God"' (14.1; 53.1). Straight-application theology would apply this straight and 'comprehensively' to the Buddha. The victims of such theology would say that the Buddha is 'a fool', since he was 'atheistic'! Such an understanding only betrays a tragi-comical superficiality in understanding religious history and culture. The Buddha, one of the greatest sages, in the company of Confucius, Lao Tse, Parmenides, Plato and Socrates, lived outside the biblical heritage. Within his own historical and cultural context he searched for the truth, he perceived it and expressed it. He never met Elijah and Isaiah. There were no radios and no paperback books then. He was a son of Indian spirituality. His lifetime ministry of forty-five years was confined to a small uneven rectangular region in north-eastern India which can be defined by lines drawn between the ancient cities of Rajagaha, Vesali, Savatthi and Baranasi. He studied human existence and its suffering with extraordinary spiritual and intellectual concentration. He realized that those 'many gods' are really of no use to the salvation of man. When he was dying at the age of eighty he told his disciples: 'Now monks, I exhort you: the components of the personality are subject to decay; exert yourselves with diligence!' In his last words to. Ananda, he said; 'Therefore, Ananda, be islands unto yourselves, a refuge unto yourselves; take the teaching as island, the teaching as refuge, have no other refuge!' (*Dighanikaya*, 16). He asked his followers not to depend on the varieties of external power, including the power that can be obtained through making sacrifice. His 'atheism' (what a straight and 'comprehensive' word!) has a remarkably similar ring to that of Socrates and the early Christians who were respectively accused of an atheistic attitude towards the traditional gods.

> ... And you see and hear that not only at Ephesus but almost throughout all Asia this Paul has persuaded and turned away a considerable company of people, saying that gods made with hands are not gods. And there is danger not only that this trade of ours may come into disrepute but also that the temple of the great goddess Artemis may count for nothing, and that she may even be deposed from her magnificence, she whom all Asia and the world worship' (Acts 19.26,27).

Paul was accused of 'atheism'! Paul was true to the biblical tradition in saying that there is no substance in the 'great goddess Artemis whom all Asia and the world worship'. Artemis is not the God of Abraham, Isaac and Jacob. She is not the Father of Jesus Christ.

The Buddha worked in a different historical situation. In that situation 'the fool says in his heart "there are gods"'. Suppose that the Buddha did say that there is *God*, that does not mean he meant the God of Abraham, Isaac and Jacob. That is what I mean by a different historical situation. There is no 'straight' relationship between the teaching of the Buddha and faith in the God of Abraham, Isaac and Jacob. There is no such 'efficient quick colonial' line between them! There are, however, many indirectly related spiritual experiences between them.

> 'Men of Athens, I perceive that in every way you are very religious. For as I passed along, and observed the objects of your worship, I found also an altar with this inscription, "To an unknown god". What therefore you worship as unknown, this I proclaim to you' (Acts. 17.22,23).

Paul did not operate his theological thinking in terms of an 'efficient quick colonial line'. He accepts this unknown god. He perceives that men of Athens are 'very religious' (so are Indians, Thais, Indonesians, Filipinos ...). He sees the presence of an indirectly related spiritual experience between what he wishes to proclaim and their 'very religious' spirituality. His theological approach is not that of a straight application, but of a rather thoughtful indirect application. 'What therefore you worship as unknown' is not condemned. On the contrary, '*this* I proclaim to you'!

I have often heard in South East Asia that Buddhism is 'anti-Christian' (what a straight and 'comprehensive' word!) because it does not teach God! Buddhism is as demonic as communism – so the proponents of the straight-application theology say – because both of them are atheistic! When and how have Christians lost the common sense of seeing that which is beautiful to be beautiful?

> Finally, brethren, whatever is honourable, whatever is just, whatever is pure, whatever is lovely, whatever is gracious, if there is any excellence, if there is anything worthy of praise, think about these things' (Phil. 4.8).

The colonial mind dislikes this apostolic advice. One finds a great deal of that which is honourable, just, pure, lovely, gracious in the history of the Buddhist as well as in Christian spirituality.

There are a number of straight-application examples that are popular among Christians in South-East Asia. I wish to take up briefly three more of them.

The first one is to do with the straight application of John 10.8. 'All who came before me are thieves and robbers; but the sheep did not heed them.' This is a strong saying indeed. Does this *all* literally mean *all*? There were many who were sent by God: Abraham, Moses, Elijah, Jeremiah, Isaiah. They came 'before me'. Obviously, if we understand 'all who came before me' as meaning the great personalities of faith in the Old Testament, then such understanding will destroy the total cohesiveness of the message of salvation given in the entire Bible, and thus erode seriously the very self-identity of Jesus as Messiah. Then, does the passage mean, for instance, the Buddha, Confucius, Socrates 'who came before me'? It is extremely hard to accept that the writer of the Gospel of John was thinking about the Buddha, Confucius and Socrates when he wrote this. Did the New Testament look at the Buddha, Confucius and Socrates as 'thieves and robbers'? I cannot imagine it did.

The passage John 10.8 must be pointing to a far more specific group of people within the context of the ministry of Jesus Christ. R.E. Brown, the biblical scholar, says:

> ... in our opinion the Pharisees and Sadducees remain the most probable targets of Jesus' remarks. The unhappy line of priestly rulers and politicians from Maccabean times until Jesus' own day could certainly be characterized as false shepherds, thieves, and robbers who came before Jesus. And the Pharisees too had soiled themselves in the political power struggle in the Hasmonean and Herodian periods. The strong language used in this explanation of the parable may well be compared with that of Matt. xxiii, where Jesus attacks the unjust exercise of authority over the people by the scribes and Pharisees.[20]

Such studied understanding of 'all who came before me' takes us closer to the understanding of the central message of the gospel of Christ than straight and 'comprehensive' application of it which really cannot make any good sense at all.

The second example has to do with Eph. 4.17-19:

> Now this I affirm and testify in the Lord, that you must no longer live as the Gentiles do, in the futility of their minds; they are darkened in their understanding, alienated from the life of God because of the ignorance that is in them, due to their hardness of heart; they have become callous and have given themselves up to licentiousness, greedy to practise every kind of uncleanness.

Shall we quickly and comprehensively look at the Gentiles in this perspective in 1975? Have all Gentiles 'given themselves up to licentiousness, greedy to practise every kind of uncleanness' in Thailand, India, the Philippines, Burma, Indonesia, Vietnam, Hong Kong, Japan, Australia, New Zealand, the Pacific Islands … ? Are they all 'alienated from the life of God'? Are they all 'greedy to practise every kind of uncleanness' who are called 'the lost two billions'? Who were the Gentiles in the mind of the writer of the epistle? Who are they in today's world? Is this the only theologically correct way of looking at the Gentiles at that time and today?

For example, are the Thais in Thailand today Gentiles? Yes, they are. They are clearly not Jews, and the great majority of them are not Christians if the Christian use of the word 'Gentile' implies 'non-Christians'. They are followers of the Buddha. If so, does this strongly negative passage apply to the Thais? Do they live 'in the futility of their minds'? Are they 'darkened in their understanding'? Are they 'alienated from the life of God'? Have they become 'callous and licentious'? Are they 'greedy to practise every kind of uncleanness'? Yes. There must be some people like that among forty million Thais. The situation must be the same with any country, be it the United Kingdom, the USSR, Japan, Germany, Indonesia, Malaysia. But can we honestly say the Gentile Fijians are 'callous and licentious' or the Gentile Burmese are 'greedy to practise every kind of uncleanness', as these passages imply? I personally find it extremely difficult to think and to feel that way. The 'Gentile' morality and spiritual life cannot be painted only in these negative terms. I have seen that all varieties of works of mercy have been done and are done in the kingdom of Thailand by the Buddhist monks. They exert their spiritual energy to combat 'greed to practise every kind of uncleanness'. The Spirit of God is working among the Gentiles (Matt. 15.21-28, Acts 10.1,2; 13.44-49).

Perhaps, then, the passages mean that 'some Gentiles' are 'greedy to practise every kind of uncleanness'. Or perhaps the writer is speaking of the terribly degenerate moral situation of the particular Gentile community which gave him a model of the Gentile life. His historical and geographical experience is naturally limited to his historical time and geographical context. The straight and comprehensive interpretation of his message causes serious missiological problems for us who work in the Asia of 1975.

If we were to understand this to mean that the moral and spiritual life of the Gentile is such 'in the eyes of God', then why are the Gentiles singled out? *All* of us are unholy in the sight of the holy God. At the same time, in this connection we must ask the question whether the God who is so concerned about history has no appreciation of the good (say, the works of mercy) done by sinful man. Does God have no interest in the 'virtue of the Gentiles'? Should all the Gentile values be condemned by the God of Abraham, Isaac and Jacob? Is God, the Father of Jesus Christ, such a condemnation-minded God?

I understand Eph. 4.17-19 to be addressed to the followers of 'the way of God' (Acts 18.26). It is not directed to the Thai Buddhists or Indonesian Muslims as we see them in 1975. There is a significant difference of historical and religious context between the Ephesians' characterization of the Gentiles and the Thai Buddhists with whom we live peacefully within the kingdom of Thailand. But I see the presence of the meaningful though indirect relationship between these

New Testament passages and *all* of us.

The third example is taken from Acts 4.12: 'And there is salvation in no one else, for there is no other name under heaven given among men by which we must be saved.' In my mind this passage and Matt. 28.19 have suffered greatly from failure to listen to them in the context of what we know of the life and ministry of Jesus Christ. This is extremely unfortunate because it means that the church in her understanding of the theology of mission failed to reflect 'christologically'. I want to discuss Matt. 28.19 in a later chapter.

Acts 4.12 is a part of Peter's witness before the rulers, elders, scribes, the high priest and high-priestly family. 'Peter, filled with the Holy Spirit, said to them ... ' (vv.5-8). This decisive and moving speech is given in only four verses! In these four verses Peter concentrates on the meaning of the name of Jesus Christ. In truth the whole apostolic message of Peter is centred on the name of Jesus.

> Rulers of the people and elders, if we are being examined today concerning a good deed done to a cripple, by what means this man has been healed, be it known to you all, and to all the people of Israel, that by the name of Jesus Christ of Nazareth (here comes a powerful apostolic summary of the Christian faith! The faith is to do with the name of Jesus Christ. What kind of the name is it?) whom you crucified, whom God raised from the dead (by this very crucified and risen name!), by him (the most fundamental identity of this 'him' is given in two words, *crucified* and *risen*) this man is standing before you well. This is the stone which was rejected by you builders (dedicated and resourceful religion-builders), but which has become the head of the corner' (v.9-11). Then comes v.12.

The only way to speak about the crucified and risen name is by participating in Christ's crucifixion and resurrection. If we wish to proclaim that 'there is salvation in no one else, for there is no other name under heaven given among men by which we must be saved', our whole life must be gripped by

this crucified and risen name as was the cripple. We bear
witness to the one who grips us, for then we *are* witness as this
once crippled man 'standing before you well'. In the context of
the Asian mission history, this dimension of the 'spirituality of
being gripped' by the name of the crucified and risen Jesus has
been suffocated by the de-spiritualized and dry 'theological'
discussion on the 'absoluteness' and 'exclusiveness' of the
name of Jesus Christ. The Asians have been taught by the
ever-resourceful missionaries and theologians that v.12 speaks
about the 'principle of exclusion'. Do you think that Peter,
who was 'filled with the Holy Spirit', just talked about
'principle of exclusion'? Peter must be speaking about the
name of the crucified and risen. He is proclaiming 'Jesus is
Lord' by the Holy Spirit (I Cor. 12.3). There is a great
difference between the 'principle of exclusion' and 'the name
of the crucified and risen one'. A principle is 'comprehensive',
predictable and tamed. Is this principle the centre of Acts 4.5-
12?

When v.12 is interpreted as a 'proof' of the 'principle of
exclusion', then in a subtle way a dry straight application of
the name of the crucified and the risen to the human situation
takes place. Straight application is abstract, not life-giving
and not edifying. It is in that sense de-spiritualized and de-
humanized application.

The name of the Buddha is an inspiring name. It stands for
the spiritual awakening, the high value of ultimate tranquility
of soul and the peaceful practise of mercy in one's community
life. It is a good name. It is an excellent name. It is a lovely
name. It is an honourable name (Phil. 4.8). Then comes the
objection! No! The name of Jesus is far better, more excellent,
lovely and honourable! We have had enough of this 'divine
beauty contest'. The name of Jesus is a good name. It is an
excellent name. It is a lovely name. It is an honourable name.
But before all these, his name is the crucified and risen name.
The crucified and risen name is not interested in entering a
'divine beauty contest'. It abhors such thought. On the
contrary, it is the name of the one who said: 'Take, eat; this is

my body.' And he took a cup, and when he had given thanks he gave it to them, saying, 'Drink of it, all of you; for this is my blood of the covenant, which is poured out for many for the forgiveness of sins" ' (Matt. 26.26-28). His name stands for the life 'poured out for many'.

But does not v.12 speak about 'exclusiveness'? Does it not say 'no one else' and 'no other name'? Are we not watering down the power of the gospel if we do not say this openly and forcefully on all occasions? The unique name of the one who 'poured out for many' must be mentioned sincerely and humbly by our life 'poured out for many'. Acts 4.12 is a high-voltage passage, particularly in present-day South East Asia. We must not approach it carelessly, lest we electrocute ourselves and others. But whose life among us has this Christ-like quality of 'poured out for many' in profound love and concern? Are we all not sinful, egotistic and self-righteous? Is there, then, any other possibility for us than to repent and ever be repentant as we think of the name of the crucified and risen one of Acts 4.12? Do we want to tell people of 'no other name'? *Do so if* our life has a quality of 'poured out for many'. *Do so if* our life is deeply that of repentance before this unique name. Otherwise, we are engaged in a de-spiritualized and de-humanized theology! Christian faith is a living reality. It takes more nourishment than straight quotations of the biblical passages. 'Not reading books or speculating, but living, dying and being damned make a theologian' (Luther).

Jesus said to the madman of the Gerasenes after he was completely restored to humanity: 'Go home to your friends, and tell them how much the Lord has done for you, and how he has had mercy on you' (Mark 5.19). For my part I prefer to speak about the mercy of the crucified and risen one among the people of Asia. This is, I have found, a much more edifying way of pointing to the 'no other name', not as an exclusive principle but as the dynamic redemptive reality of the love of God. I make a distinction between an unnecessary stumbling block and a genuine stumbling block. The former we

constantly create. The latter is given to us and we have no
control over it. The straight application of Acts 4.12 has
created a variety of unnecessary stumbling blocks. Only rarely
has this passage become a genuine stumbling block.

The truth that the Bible speaks to us is a saving truth. This
saving truth is a mediated truth. The mediator's name is Jesus
Christ, the crucified and risen. ' ... there is one mediator
between God and men, the man Christ Jesus, who gave
himself as a ransom for all ... ' (I Tim. 2.5,6). The biblical
truth is not an *intact* truth but a *suffered* truth. The truth suffers
because it is deeply *in contact* with man. No handle on the
cross! Jesus carries the cross. He speaks to us at the depth of
our existence. He invites us to take up the cross without a
handle. A 'comprehensive and straight' mentality must be
challenged by the crucified mind.

' ... while he was yet at a distance, his father saw him and
had compassion and ran and embraced him and kissed him'
(Luke 15.20). The prodigal son just stood there. He was
embraced and kissed by the father. When the son stood and
the father embraced – the son experienced the saving truth
holding him firmly.

8 The Spat-upon Jesus Christ

'... kneeling before him they mocked him ... they spat upon him ... ' (Matt. 27.28-31).

The 'spat-upon finality' of Jesus Christ points to 'spat-upon bishops', 'spat-upon theology', 'spat-upon evangelism', 'spat-upon combat against racism', 'spat-upon churches' ...

The word 'finality' frightens me. Once I gave an ambitious lecture in Thailand on the 'finality of Jesus Christ'. I translated this technical expression into Thai, meaning 'Jesus Christ the Last One' or 'Jesus Christ as the One who appeared last'. I drew a parallel between Jesus Christ and the King of Thailand. Both of them are the Last Ones, meaning that they are 'final' personalities. My good congregation thought that Christianity and the monarchy were in their last hour of existence! Soon they objected, saying that the King is not the Last One but the First One; he is not the Last Person but the First Person. So I had, on the spot, to change 'finality' into 'primacy'. My poor theological structure and the set of Thai sentences which I prepared conscientiously the night before were all confused.

My Asian friends are willing to listen to the story of Rom. 5.6,7: 'While we were yet helpless, at the right time Christ died for the ungodly. Why, one will hardly die for a righteous man – though perhaps for a good man one will dare even to die. But God shows his love for us in that while we were yet sinners Christ died for us.' They are happy to hear Matthew 5.45: ' ... he makes his sun rise on the evil and on the good, and sends rain on the just and on the unjust.' The Bible is full of fascinating Asian stories. All these stories invite us to come to 'the fragrance of the knowledge of him' (II Cor. 2.14). But if the Christian message is formulated into a chauvinistic Christianity, that is, a 'superiority Christianity', 'the-best-religion Christianity', and 'finality Christianity', then they at once detect arrogance, superficiality and unreligiousness in *our* understanding of Christianity.

To say that Christianity is a superior religion compared with other religions, such as Buddhism, Hinduism and Islam, is like insisting that Japanese cuisine is *superior* to Indian or British cuisine. The word 'superior' is misplaced here. It is hastily used. Instead one should say that Japanese cuisine (raw tuna sliced and placed on steaming rice) is *different* from American cuisine (mashed potato, turkey drumstick and gravy). For my part, I love sliced raw tuna. But that does not mean that Japanese cuisine is superior to American cuisine. They are different. 'Superior' is a comparative concept. This car is better (superior) than that car. Presumably, then, one must be able to compare 'objectively' (!) the great religions of the world and decide which one is the superior one to which one. 'But before we compare, we must thoroughly know what we compare.' (Max Müller, *Letter to Renan*, 1883). In order to achieve such an enormous assignment, one must not only have a vast knowledge and profound religious experience in relation to these religions, but must also stand at the top of Mount Olympus to make a solemn declaration that one is superior or the *best* one. None of us is equal to such a superhuman task. And in fact such an enterprise is senseless and useless as we live a religiously committed life. One can compare cars. But to compare the living reality of religious truth and life is a different story.

That Gautama Buddha has much to do with today's Buddhism is a fact. That the man called Jesus lived some two thousand years ago in the corner of the Roman Empire is a fact. That Muhammad was born in AD 570 is a fact. We can multiply such facts to a great extent. But religious life is not founded on the aggregates of these facts. It roots itself in something deeper than all the facts. This 'something deeper' refuses to be compared 'objectively'. Religious commitment belongs to the world of 'I-Thou-relationship' (I and the Buddha, I and *Allah*) and not 'I-It-relationship' (I and desk, I and car), to put it in the language of Martin Buber. 'It' can be comparatively treated. 'Thou' cannot be. I can compare this 'it' with that 'it'. But I am confronted by a completely different situation when I wish to compare this 'thou' with that 'thou'. I can 'handle' the former situation, while the latter I cannot, since it points to the relationship of encounter, meaning and commitment. The Buddhist believes in the Buddha. He encounters the Buddha as his 'Thou'. Religious faith cannot be 'it-ized'. That which refuses to be 'it-ized' cannot be objectively compared.

It can however, be subjectively compared. 'Subjective comparison' does not do justice to the concept of comparison. Such comparison *usually* becomes a self-centred and self-important observation of other religious faiths. Self-importance is incongruous with the crucified mind. To say that 'all the religions except Christianity are inferior faiths' is a quick and 'efficient' judgment. But it is not an observation made by the crucified mind. For centuries Christians, without studying about the people of the great *shemas*, made a quick judgment and simply pronounced that Christianity is superior to the other religions. This has done more harm than good for Christian evangelism.

To the Buddhists 'there is no other name but the Buddha', for the Christians 'there is no other name but Christ', for the Muslim 'there is no other name but Muhammad'. Such a spiritual situation of commitment cannot be described and systematized by comparative words such as 'superior' and 'best'. The Christian faith would lose nothing if Christians stopped calling their faith the superior or the best religion. These words are, like the armour of Saul on David (I Sam. 17.38,39), not useful for the spiritual life of the church.

One day a missionary friend of mine carefully presented for my benefit his arguments for the superiority of Christianity. He said that Christianity is superior to Hinduism because the latter has lots of idols while Christianity does not! He was emphatic in pointing out that some of the Hindu idols are extremely grotesque. It is self-evident, my friend argued, that the religion which teaches the worship of the true living God is superior to the religion that teaches allegiance to the idols. I was deeply impressed by his sincerity. But I am still unhappy about using the word 'superior' in this context. From the Christian viewpoint, idol worship (with a Christian definition of worship and idol) is an unwholesome religious practice, and therefore 'inferior'. But from the Hindu viewpoint (with a Hindu definition of worship and idol), it is a wholesome religious practice, and therefore not an 'inferior' religious activity at all. There is a difference of religious history and experience between them. Christians may say that such Hindu definitions of worship and idol are themselves wrong. But to be Hindu means to be at home with the Hindu religious experience and its expressions. From an Islamic viewpoint the use of images in Christian churches is evidence of an idolatrous mentality.

In Jesus Christ, God came to us with his final plan, final seriousness, final demonstration of love, final sacrifice – this is what Christians confess in faith. This story which theologians technically express in the phrase 'the finality of Christ' must be told as a story by the story-oriented crucified mind. That is what Jesus did!

> Now when John heard in prison about the deeds of the Christ, he sent word by his disciples and said to him, 'Are you he who is to come, or shall we look for another?' And Jesus answered them, 'Go and tell John what you hear and see: the blind receive their sight and the lame walk, lepers are cleansed and the deaf hear, and the dead are raised up, and the poor have good news preached to them. And blessed is he who takes no offence at me' (Matt. 11.2-6).

John the Baptist was in prison. From prison he sent an inquiry to Jesus asking if he was the one who is to come. John was confined. He was suffering. He must have felt a deep disillusionment and disappointment in his mission. He must have felt that the darkness was thickening around him fast. He desperately needed to know whether Jesus was indeed the one who is to come. His whole life and mission depended on the answer to this one question. Yes. He had introduced Jesus. 'I have been sent before him. ... He must increase, but I must decrease' (John 3.28,30). Within the prison walls, he had heard about the activity of Jesus and now he wished to have the word of Jesus addressed to him. The answer of Jesus was straightforward. He describes the coming reality of the Messianic age. The message concludes with this one significant sentence: 'Blessed is he who takes no offence at me.' It is important to know that the question of the finality of Christ was first asked by the prisoner within the wall of prison! Discussions on this subject conducted in an air-conditioned university library or in the carpeted lounge of a theological seminary will become meaningful only when they are related to this primary context of 'theology within prison'.

He is the one to come. How do you know? 'Go and tell John what you hear and see.' The amazing divine restoration, re-integration and healing of man are taking place! Then is it self-evident that Jesus is the one who is to come? Self-evident? No! Not at all. There are always many who take offence at him (who stumble at him). Jesus does not force those who stumble at him into the faith. He says only 'blessed are they ... ' 'Go and tell John what you *hear* and *seek*.' This is ordinary *hearing* and *seeing* which contain an extraordinary dimension. Do you hear? Do you see? 'Blessed are you ... ' The 'finality of Jesus Christ' cannot be *proved*, even with a hundred powerful quotations from the Bible. It is not a thought or position which can be established by way of 'objective proofs'. It belongs to the domain of 'blessed are they ... '. It takes place when our ordinary hearing and seeing are penetrated by an extraordinary hearing and seeing! 'And he said, "He who has ears to hear, let him hear"' (Mark 4.9). This is the way that Jesus himself conducted, if I may be awkward, the 'finality of Christ' discussion.

You remember Joseph's dream? How his sheaf stood up?

Up to now the discussion of the finality of Christ has been predominantly formulated within the framework of Joseph's sweet dream of my-sheaf-stood-up theology. All other religions are supposed to bow down to the upright sheaf of Christianity. Often this thinking has been bolstered by paternalistic-colonial sentiment and language. For example, we hear even in 1975 (!) from the mouths of the proponents of the finality of Jesus Christ that the Asians cannot know the meaning of moral living without the missionaries' Christian instruction! Christians today do not realize how deeply they are still dreaming the pleasing dream of Joseph. That Jesus Christ is the one who is promised to come is a crucified truth. It is not an ordinary truth which can be established by comparative studies. 'But far be it from me to glory except in the cross of our Lord Jesus Christ, by which the world has been crucified to me, and I to the world' (Gal. 6.14). This new self-identity, originating in the 'cross of our Lord Jesus Christ', points to the one who is promised to come. The crucified truth must be proclaimed by the crucified mind.

'Where two or three are gathered in my name, there am I in the midst of them' (Matt. 18.20). This is the promise given not only to the church but to all the missiological situations in Thailand, Hong Kong and Switzerland, and so on. 'In my name' is the name of the one who suffered. 'There is no other name' means the name of the one who suffered. ' ... kneeling before him they mocked him, ... they spat upon him, ... stripped him of the robe ...' (Matt. 27.28-31). If Jesus Christ was mocked, spat upon and stripped, then his 'finality' is mocked, spat upon and stripped. The 'mocked finality' is, then, the christological finality. But 'the mocked finality' and 'spat-upon finality' do not come under an ordinary concept of finality or primacy.

Jesus is 'the one who is to come', 'there is no other name ... ' and 'where two or three are gathered in my name ... ' point to Jesus Christ who saves the one who mocks him, who cleans the one who spits upon him. The finality of Jesus Christ – what an unusual concept of finality! – grasps us instead of being articulated by us. Church and mission together draw their life from *this name*. The spat-upon Jesus means the spat-upon finality of Jesus. It must mean then the 'spat-upon bishops', 'spat-upon theology', 'spat-upon evangelism', 'spat-upon "combat-against-racism"', 'spat-upon churches'. The finality of Christ and 'being spat-upon' go together! The glory of Christ and 'being spat-upon' go together! Such a concept of finality is in diametrical opposition to the paternalistic mentality. If there is one thing that paternalism cannot take that is this being spat upon.

'To be apostolic' means 'to be ready to be spat upon'. 'We have become, and are now, as the refuse of the world, the off-scouring of all things' (I Cor. 4.13). History can be approached in two ways: the way of spitting upon others and the way of being spat upon by others. History is touched superficially by the former and profoundly by the latter. Ecclesiology and missiology must be rooted in the latter, since the first-born of all things and the first-born of the dead came to us in the latter way. I maintain that to the degree that the church has spat upon other religious faiths and spiritual traditions in Asia, she has become superficial in her christological impact upon the Asian man and history. To the degree that the church has been spat upon, she has become alive in mission and healing in the history.

Jesus before Pilate puzzles us. 'And the chief priests accused him of many things. And Pilate again asked him, "Have you no answer to make? See how many charges they bring against you". But Jesus made no further answer, so that Pilate wondered.' (Mark 15.3-5). Wasn't this an opportunity for Jesus to speak out in his own defence and that of his mission? He remained silent. 'In the beginning was the Word.' This very Word acted as though 'in the beginning was the silence'. At Caesarea Philippi 'he strictly charged the disciples to tell no one that he was the Christ'. This again puzzles us. Why not tell the saving truth to everyone? Is not this an indication Jesus dislikes his 'finality' to be talked about noisily?

Discussions of 'finality', 'superiority' and 'the best religion is Christianity' are motivated by the mind trying to speak about Jesus Christ on the basis of a 'comprehensive' observation. The concepts of finality, superiority and the best presuppose the result of a comprehensive assessment. But theological perception is primarily grace-grasped instead of data-grasped. No handle on the cross! Theological language is symbolical, sacramental and revelatory instead of being comprehensive and comparative. It is so because 'no one has ever seen God; the only Son, who is in the bosom of the Father, he has made him known' (John 1.18). If we should speak on the 'finality' of Jesus Christ, we must know that it is the 'mocked finality', 'hidden finality' and 'crucified finality'. The only Son made God known to us as he gave himself for us.

Let me relate the theology of 'mocked finality' to South East Asian life. The South East Asian traditional style of life, the sense of value, the manner of conducting human relationships, education, transportation, political organization and so on are being disrupted by both positive and negative values which Western civilization has brought in. In this critical-historical moment, South East Asian peoples are engaged in two areas of immense theological importance. Let me express this in New Testament language: they are, first, in the area of 'Come out of the man, you unclean spirit!' (Mark 5.8), and secondly, in the area of 'man shall not live by bread alone, but by every word that proceeds from the mouth of God' (Matt. 4.4; Deut. 8.3).

The poverty-stricken and labour-exploited masses of South-East Asia are shouting: 'Come out of the nation, you unclean spirits of corruption, oppression, exploitation and inflation!' The works of the unclean spirit are unmistakably there when corruption paralyses national economy and morality. A twenty-year-old woman, working ten hours a day, draws only five Singapore dollars a day. The rich are getting richer through the sacrifice of the human dignity of the masses. 'Come out of the man, you unclean spirit!' No other passage can be closer to the minds of the frustrated masses. They experience that the unclean spirit is powerful and does not come out easily. But the masses refuse to stop saying 'Come out ... ' They 'hope against hope' in the midst of enormous frustration. Here is a reality of 'Christian civilization' which is completely different from the traditional civilization of Christendom. When the masses shout for the exorcism of the unclean spirit, are they not participating in the exorcism of Jesus Christ? Is not this a sign of a great spiritual struggle and awakening? When they say 'Come out of the man, you unclean spirit!' to their exploiters – yes, brutal exploiters – are they not pointing to Jesus Christ, even though they are not aware of his name? Yes. They are not aware of the name of Jesus Christ. But his name is there and his name is the name of the crucified one. This name, the mocked name, spat-upon name is – how remarkable and how strange! – the name that exorcises the evil names. It is mocked by the evil power, yet – or rather because of it! – it is able to stand against the power of evil and make it captive (II Cor. 10.3-5). The mocked name is the very name by which the evil names are cast out!

Modernization is ambiguous in its impact upon the people of South East Asia. It is both 'stone' and 'bread' (Matt. 7.9). The masses have taken notice of the 'bread' character of the impact of modernization. Newly available means of transportation can take a sick child to a hospital fifteen kilometres away, even in the rain. It is 'bread'. Ubiquitous Japanese transistor radios keep the masses informed about economic, political, racial, technological and domestic-international situations. It is 'bread'. Their intake of information has been phenomenally increased. Efficient printing machines placed good quality textbooks in the hands of the millions of South East Asian children. Education has been universalized and upgraded. It is again newly baked 'bread'. Technology has brought running water into kitchens. Telephones eradicated the distances. The people in South East Asia are now beginning to taste the newly-baked modernization 'bread' of all kinds.

The newly baked 'bread' is placed in the context of 'man shall not live by bread alone, but by every word that proceeds

from the mouth of God'. Each cultural context of humanity
has its own 'word that proceeds from the mouth of God'.
Sometimes, it is the voice of human conscience or consensus of
the elders of the community. At other times, it is the
fundamental creed of Buddhism or Islam, and so on. In each
living context, the newly baked 'bread' is examined. How does
it stand up to 'every word that proceeds from the mouth of
God'? 'Bread alone' is not enough. 'Bread alone' is even
dangerous to the welfare of the human spirituality. 'Clothing
alone' becomes obscene and perverse. 'Shelter alone' becomes
spiritually wasteful 'grand-house-prestige-ism'. 'Sex alone'
becomes paralysing sexism. 'Money alone' becomes anti-
human exploitative egoism. 'Brain alone' becomes dangerous
idolatry of human intelligence. 'Work alone' becomes a
system of self-imposed slavery. 'Technology alone' becomes a
threat to human life. 'Power alone' becomes destructive power
which produces a repressive society. 'Religion alone' becomes
a self-righteous human relationship. Bread, clothing, shelter,
sex, money, brain, work, technology, power and religion must
be illuminated and judged by 'every word that proceeds from
the mouth of God'. I am saying that this is happening apart
from the explicit biblical word of God. While the people of
South East Asia engage in this 'bread alone ... ' dispute they
do not consciously associate the name of Jesus Christ. Yet it is
a deeply biblical theological discussion, since it has to do with
the basic welfare of humanity upon this planet. The name of
Jesus Christ is there. It is not confessed in faith. But it is there.
Where? In all these concrete situations of human life, Jesus
Christ is profoundly there since it is impossible to stop the one
whose name is spat-upon finality from coming and being
there. It is possible to stop him *if* his name stands simply for
'finality' (my-sheaf-stood-in-the-centre). But no one can
obstruct the way of the mocked and spat-upon Lord. The
spat-upon Lord is the universal Lord! No situation can
frighten him.

'Now the tax collectors and sinners were all drawing near to
hear him. And the Pharisees and the scribes murmured,

saying, "This man receives sinners and eats with them"'
(Luke 15.1,2). He reveals his own kind of 'finality' as he 'eats
with them'. Should we establish his finality by way of
comparison? By way of some theological proofs? It is not our
business to establish his finality for him. 'For who has known
the mind of the Lord, or who has been his counsellor?' (Rom.
11.34). We are caught by the power of the living Lord. Our
foundation of faith is infinitely more secure since we have not
laid it. The spat upon finality is the crucified finality. In his
suffering finality (cross) we find the possibility of our life
renewed and resurrected. It has come to us! We have not
created it! No handle on the cross!

9 Is Christianity History-minded?

The relationship between story-theology and theory-theology.

A teacher-complex erodes the Christian sense of history.

'The impartiality of God' stressed in the inter-religious situation draws Christianity down to history.

Don't just 'go', but 'go, therefore ... '

Is Christ crucified or is Christ crucifying others?

In repentance we become deeply historical.

Let us imagine ourselves in Bangkok (the city of heavenly beings) tonight. We are sitting in one of the street-corner Chinese restaurants. Let's have a dish of 20 bahts *pat-mu-priaw-wan* (sweet and sour pork) and bowls of steamed rice. Over this 'dialectical' dish (sweet yet sour, sour yet sweet – what a mysterious taste!) we may have a straight talk on theology and ministry in South East Asia. I know one or two mosquitoes will fly into my big mouth while I talk! It has happened before.

Strangely, and I am sure it will surprise you to hear it, I am finding that Christianity is not interested in history. When I was a theological student, my textbooks and my teachers bombarded me with the idea that Christianity is an intensely historical religion. It is a history-rooted faith. It is faith in the Exodus God who is concerned with history. Jesus Christ, the historical man, is God incarnate. In Jesus of Nazareth, God's ultimate saving intention has been realized in history. I think my textbooks and my teachers were right. If we take away the historical dimension from the Christian faith, we take the blood out of the living body.

The Christian faith is rooted in history. It is very much so because Jesus Christ was the crucified and spat-upon Lord.

Yet the religion called Christianity can behave otherwise. What I see and experience today in Asia impresses me that Christianity is neither concerned about history nor trying to understand what 'the faith rooted in history' means. Christianity has touched the history of Asia only superficially. It has not really been spat upon by the Asians as the Christ was spat upon by the Roman soldiers.

What is history? I do not find myself competent to define it. I cannot put history on my table and look at it as a medical researcher can scrutinize experimental rats. History strikes me as different from the wiring inside a television set. I feel that history is living, unpredictable and constantly moving between hope and despair. History is a biographical story. It is fundamentally a story rather than a theory. I understand that the Bible has to do with story and not theory. The biblical God is a story-God, not a theory-God. History can be a story so long as it is not carried around by a handle. Exactly at this point I find the mystery and excitement of history.

For the last fifteen years the South East Asians have lived under the spell of an unchallengeable secular theory ('Made in USA') on their history, called the 'domino theory'. If South Vietnam goes to Communism, then next will be Cambodia, Laos, Thailand, Malaysia, Indonesia, as the dominoes go. This is a forceful argument, because it has put a firm handle to history. I am not prepared to say that this theory is nonsense. But what the theory has produced historically in South East Asia is a paralysing moral degeneration in South East Asian capitals: pervasive corruption, brutal exploitation of the people, outright denial of human rights, successive emergence of totalitarian governments, controlled education. The domino theory does not commend itself. The 'domino theory' silenced a great deal of 'living stories', and the American dollars 'dominoed' all the way to the Swiss Banks under the 'big names' of the governments.

Asia has its history (story). Christianity (not Jesus Christ) approached this story and often put a handle to it and tried to carry it around at will. The Asian story has been dealt with as a theory by the theory-minded. When the story is treated as a theory, it loses its life. Christian life and Christian doctrine must make an integral unit. But the life, the story, must be first; the theory only clarifies, throws light on, the story. The theory must be rooted in the historical and cultural context of the story. The Japanese theory of flower-arrangement comes out of continuous experience with the flower. The British theory of democracy is deeply anchored in their long experience of democratic history (story). When a foreign theory is imposed upon a story, obviously the story suffers. If I hazard a generalization at this point, I would say that today Asia is experiencing an intense conflict between Western theory, historically vigorous, and Asian story. In the area of mission, this means that certain Western mission theories have been used to mould the Asian Christian experience. Asians have been asked to depart from their own historical and cultural contexts. Asian Christians are often culturally deformed or even cultural monsters in their own historical community! It is true that such experience, though painful, is stimulating. Pain and stimulation are inter-related concepts. But that does not excuse a careless and aggressive imposition of foreign theory upon the Asian story. I must point out how deeply responsible all kinds of denominational theories have been in creating such historical alienation among the Asian Christians.

I must be quick to point out that the history of Christianity in Asia has not been wholly 'handled' this way. There have been moving stories of the 'non-handle' crucified-mind missiology. A great number of Asians have found in Jesus Christ the One who denied himself for the sake of others. The Asian story and the story of Jesus Christ met and fused as the Jamuna River flows into the mighty Ganges River. Asian stories are listened to as stories. The Christ-story is listened to as a story. And the two stories have come into a confluence. But unfortunately, theory often attacked the story in the history of Asian Christianity and Asians themselves are also responsible. The theory-mind is 'wise' and 'strong'. It is 'resourceful'. It is symbolized by the highly nourishing lunch-box. It is competent to 'handle' mission situations, and it has so many 'correct' answers and procedures that it has become uninteresting to the people. If Christianity were seriously concerned with history, it would have listened to the stories of the Asian peoples and thus would become a most *interesting* faith among the Asian peoples.

Secondly, the 'wise' and 'strong' Christianity wants to teach. It does not want to learn. Since it does not want to learn from the people, it has become a less historical religion. Education is a strongly historical process. ' ... God has led you these forty years in the wilderness, that he might humble you, testing you to know what was in your heart, whether you would keep his commandments, or not' (Deut. 8.2). If religion stands outside the educational process, it begins to assume an uncanny a-historical character. Such Christianity is 'efficient', yet in the eyes of the spat-upon Lord perhaps quite 'inefficient'! The greater the distance from history, the more 'efficient' will be the behaviour of Christianity. That 'God's weakness is stronger than men and God's foolishness is wiser than men' (I Cor. 1.25) means that God's experience of history is far deeper than ours. The greater the penetration into history, the less 'efficient' will be the acts of Christianity. Missiologically speaking, 'efficiency' can often betray a superficial sense of history and thus the mind of *idolatry*. It is idolatrous to bring the concepts of spirituality and efficiency into one melting pot (Exod. 32.24). The 'truth' which tends to work efficiently at our command is most likely an untruth (idol).

When the Thai Buddhists are paying their respects to the image of the Buddha in the Marble Temple in Bangkok, they are not engaged in idolatry. If you think they are, then your theology is too efficient. There is a centuries-long history of religious experience behind the Buddhist act of paying respect. Idolatry is more subtle than 'bowing the head three times'. 'God, I thank thee that I am not like other men, extortioners, unjust, adulterers, or even like this tax

collector. ...' (Luke 18.11). The name of God is mentioned.
God's name here does not mean, however, judgment and
salvation. The 'I' of 'I thank thee' is more central than 'thee'.
Is not this idolatrous? Is he not too efficient in establishing his
position before God? Does he not combine spirituality and
efficiency 'in the name of God'? Is not this idolatry, since it is
only before idols that man can combine spirituality and
efficiency without hesitation? Is not this man suffering from a
'teacher-complex'? Is he not giving theological lessons to God?
Is he not an efficient lecturer to God? Like this man, the
Christianity that suffers from a 'teacher-complex' cannot
really go deeply into the history in which the people live with
their own stories. Efficiency, idolatry and the teacher-complex
are thus interrelated. One of the major Protestant
denominations has this to say about its 1975 world-wide
mission: 'To initiate a world-wide mission and evangelism
offensive.' 'Evangelism offensive' is a strange 'Christian'
expression indeed! To whom is the offensive directed? To
those who are 'overseas'? To the heathen? Is this great
denomination still thinking of evangelism in terms of an
'offensive'? Is Jesus Christ 'on a tree' (Gal. 3.13) or is he in the
Pentagon? What is evangelism other than pointing to the
crucified Lord (Gal. 3.1)? Can anyone make an 'offensive'
out of the one who 'was publicly portrayed as crucified'? I
sense here evidence of a militant teacher-complex which has
made Christianity in Asia historically superficial and docetic.

(Let's have some more rice. How about 7-ups? Do you
know why zoology has not developed in China? Chinese
people here tell me that it is because they are more interested
in cooking than in studying the animal! So here we are with
some more sweet-and-sour pork!)

Thirdly, Christianity is a religion. You may protest against
this. 'All right!', you may say, 'If Christianity is a religion, it is
a genuine and true religion over against other misguided, false
and man-made religions. Christianity is a faith in the living
God in Christ and therefore not a religion in an ordinary
sense!' Please remember that Christianity is not identical with

Jesus Christ. A Christian is not Jesus Christ. Christians are supposed to be 'Christ-like'. But they are only rarely so. Whether we are discouraged or irritated, it is a fact. A house of bishops does not necessarily mean a house of 'Christ-like' bishops. There is a distance between Jesus Christ and Christianity as we know it. 'Not everyone who says to me "Lord, Lord" shall enter into the kingdom of heaven, but he who does the will of my Father who is in heaven' (Matt. 7.21). The religion in which Jesus Christ is called 'Lord, Lord' is Christianity. But it is very possible that the Christians (who call Jesus Christ 'Lord, Lord') do not do 'the will of my Father'. In Paul's letter to the Corinthians, which was written about AD 53 and 54, the apostle spoke about divisions within the church (I Cor. 1.10-17). Division within the church is obviously not 'the will of my Father'. Christianity is a historically developed religion, just as Hinduism, Buddhism and Islam are. There is no such thing as a divine, pure and uncontaminated Christianity. As a religion, Karl Barth says, Christianity with other religions must stand under the judgment of the Gospel of Christ. 'There will be tribulation and distress for every human being who does evil, the Jew first and also the Greek, but glory and honour and peace for everyone who does good, the Jew first and also the Greek. For God shows no partiality' (Rom. 2.9-11).

I see you do not like Rom. 2.9-11. You think, may I guess, that this message of God's impartiality is only a part of theological preparation for the real salvation theology, namely, the doctrine of justification by faith (Rom. 3.21). You may be right that the heart of Paul's message is found in justification by faith and not in God's impartiality. But I have seen in the life of theology and ministry, in Asia (as well as in the West), the doctrine of justification by faith losing all its original (Mohammed Ali-like) punches. Perhaps this 'prince of all doctrines' (Luther) and the mind of the Asian civilization do not make a creative combination. The doctrine of justification by faith needs a strong sense of the righteousness of God as a backdrop in order to make itself

meaningful. I do not think such a theological experience of the
righteousness of God is historically a part of the mind of our
civilization. But now ... it is coming! It is coming in the form
of the impartiality of God. I have seen that when Christians
take God's impartiality seriously – unfortunately this happens
rarely – the doctrine of justification by faith begins to speak its
Asian meaning. But when they ignore the impartial character
of God – 'there will be tribulation and distress for every
human being (whatever his religious commitment is) who
does evil (whatever his religious commitment is)' – the
doctrine of justification by faith has then become empty talk.
The impartiality of God is the righteousness of God. He is
righteous because he is impartial. The significant point is that
this awareness of the impartiality of God has emerged within
the church as a result of its being caught within the inter-
religious situation of Asia. The people of the other living faiths
are demanding that the Asian Christians take the impartiality
of the Christian God seriously. *They* are saying that Christian
authenticity must be rooted in the sense of the impartiality of
God. I believe that they are making a historic contribution to
the Christian faith. They are placing the churches in Asia in a
creative Asian context in which they can come to a deeper and
genuine appreciation of the doctrine of 'justification by faith'
in Asia. If we want to maintain a strong Rom. 3.21, we must
maintain a strong Rom. 2.9-11. In the latter are the bricks
which build the former. The inter-religious situation is urging
the Asian Christians to enter an Asian version of an
'Augustinian monastery', if I put my point in the language of
the time of Luther.

In the inter-religious situation, the impartiality of God is
not an abstract theological concept. A historical inter-
religious situation is here with us today. Christians meet
Buddhists, Muslims work with Hindus and Buddhists'
children attend Christian schools. The Christian church has
an opportunity to demonstrate her rootedness in history by
rejecting 'my-sheaf-stood-up-theology' and being confronted
by the historical judgment of the impartiality of God. The

theological message which we hear from the inter-religious situation is the impartiality of God. An act of mercy is an act of mercy in whatever name it is done. Refusing to accept bribery is a righteous act in whatever name it is refused. To take care of the wounded person is commendable in whatever name it is done. As long as the churches in Asia ignore the impartiality of God, they remain irresponsible to history.

In the concrete context of history, Christianity is a religion among religions: Christians may not think so, but those who do not profess the Christian faith think so. There is only one way by which it can be demonstrated that Christianity is a profound religion to the eyes of the adherents of the other faiths; that is by the life style of being 'poured out for many'. Such self-denial – the Christlike self-denial – is *deeply religious and therefore deeply historical*. At this point history and religion intersect in the eyes of the peoples of other faiths and the world.

We have studied the Buddhist *shema*. The third truth of the Four Noble Truths is this: 'But what, O monks, is the noble truth of the Extinction of suffering? It is the complete fading away and extinction of this craving, its forsaking and giving up, liberation and detachment from it.' Christian theologians make haste to say that this is an invitation to go 'beyond history' and to 'detachment from history'. Christianity, they insist, stands for going 'into history' and being 'attached to history'. It is true that there is a contrast between the faith of 'in the beginning was the Word' and the faith of 'in the beginning was Tranquillity'. My immediate concern at this juncture is that often Christians fail to see the *historical* efforts the Buddhists demonstrate in order to achieve the value of 'beyond history' and 'detachment from history'. This 'historicity' of the Buddhist spiritual exercises is often more impressive than the 'historicity' of the Christian spiritual exercise to achieve the value of 'into history' and 'attachment to history'. In Thailand, Burma and Sri Lanka, if the Christians exert as much 'historical effort' – for instance, self-denial – as the Buddhists do, Christianity will certainly be able to present itself as a 'historical' faith. 'Historicity of religious efforts' is one of the critical points at which the judgment and hope of the impartiality of God work. The doctrine of justification by faith divorced from the teaching of the impartiality of God is too 'wise' and too 'strong'! The crucified mind does not feel at home with such triumphalism, irresponsible to, and uprooted from, history.

A Christianity which ignores the impartiality of God naturally fails to see our history in the Christian perspective. It sees history – particularly the history of other religions – in the perspective of its self-assertiveness. It does not see history in the perspective of self-denial. I do not think Christianity in Asia for the last four hundred years has really listened to the people. It has ignored the people. It has ignored the spirituality of the people. It has ignored the people's deep aspiration and frustration. It has ignored and even condemned the people's moral strivings and sensitivities. In short, it has ignored God, who asks 'where are you'? It has listened to its bishops, theologians and financial sponsors eight thousand miles away. In contrast Jesus sought help from a Samaritan woman: 'Give me a drink' (John 4.7). 'What is your name?' Jesus asked a madman (Mark 5.9). 'Zacchaeus, make haste and come down (from that high place with a good 'comprehensive' view. Up there you may think you know how to 'handle' the situation. But actually I am down here holding you in a way you do not understand. Now hold the branch firmly as I tell you that I need you) for I must stay at your house today' (give me lodging! give me your hospitality! give me your protection under your roof!).

The teacher-complex tends to be powered by a one-way-traffic psychology. This one-way set-up has been justified by the use of the command of the Risen Lord: 'Go, therefore, and make disciples of all nations, baptizing them in the name of the Father and of the Son and of the Holy Spirit, teaching them to observe all that I have commanded ... ' (Matt. 28.19,20). I do not understand this powerful sentence, however, as an approval for 'one-way traffic'. I believe that it

is only through 'Christlike-going' (please take note that it is
not just 'go', but 'go therefore ... '. That is to say, 'go' on the
basis of the life and ministry of Jesus Christ, his love, his self-
denial, his hope, his death, his resurrection ...) that we are to
'make disciples of all nations'. The Christlike going is a
'difficult going'. It is a painful going. It is a going in which one
encounters the cross. It is a going in which one must carry the
cross even without knowing how to carry it. 'He saved others;
he cannot save himself' (Matt. 27.42). Precisely this is his
manner of 'going'! His going is a going in which he does not
save himself.

Then we must read Matt. 28.19,20 together with Matt.
27.41,42 and with Matthew 16.24,25. The Great Commission
is misunderstood when 'go' and 'therefore' are separated. The
crusading mind can find its theologically positive role when it
is guided by 'go therefore', but when it heeds the 'go' alone,
then it becomes the mind against the mind of Christ, the
primary model of the crucified mind. 'Go therefore' will touch
our history in the way Jesus Christ touched. 'But God shows
his love for us in that while we were yet sinners Christ died for
us' (Rom. 5.8). This is the way God showed his love and
'respect' to history.

Let me quote from the recent writing of an American
missiologist:

In the 1974 meeting of the American Society of Missiology
at Wheaton College, a panel discussed the contemporary
missionary situation in Brazil. At one point a certain
missiologist was quoted as having said that if all 3,000
foreign missionaries were removed from Brazil tomorrow,
the Christian community there would scarcely notice they
were gone and the churches would probably continue to
grow at the same rate. Tongue-in-cheek, Edward Dayton of
Missions Advance Research and Communications
(MARC), a panel member, spoke up and said, 'I would
disagree with that figure. My own observations would
confirm that only 2,800 of them could be so removed!'

Dayton, of course, drew a hearty laugh from the audience, but most of us had the uneasy feeling that deep down it was nervous laughter. Are 2,800 of 3,000 missionaries to Brazil really that unproductive?[21]

I find myself readily in agreement with Mr Dayton. A missionary career in Asia is almost invariably an envious one, being comfortably surrounded by all kinds of securities. To be missionary means to enjoy a life-long safe distance from the precariousness of life. But this is not the most important issue about missionary vocation. The issue is not an economic but a theological one. To my mind this disturbing remark of Mr Dayton shows how easy it is to 'go', but how difficult it is to 'go therefore'. In the living tradition of the Bible only those who 'go therefore' can be called 'productive missionaries'.

The November 1974 issue of *Listener*, the most popular New Zealand magazine, carries a poem of Albert Leomala, a New Hebridean:

> Cross run away, Run away from me.
> I hate you. Take your ideas
> And your civilization
> And go back
> To where you belong.

The New Hebridean speaks here for millions not only in the Pacific but in the East. For them, powerful Western civilization has destroyed many cherished human values. This observation of course needs to be subjected to urgent and careful examination. But the point to which I wish to call your attention is about the first word in this poem of outbursting anger – *Cross!* Mr Leomala is not denouncing the Western civilization symbolized by factory-chimney pollution, concrete buildings and pavements, speedy-human relationship and hard-cash power. He sees the symbol of hated Western civilization in the cross! I thought the cross of Jesus Christ could not have an enemy. I thought that it would be impossible to take a hate-stand against the symbol of self-denial, the life 'poured out'. How can anyone in his right mind hate the one who emptied himself (Phil. 2.4-8)? Is Jesus Christ then presented as the crucifying Lord instead of the crucified Lord? If he did crucify others, then the hate expressed against the cross is understandable.

In truth Christians have preached Jesus Christ crucified. But have the Asians and the people in the Pacific experienced Jesus Christ as bulldozing and crucifying them? That the Christ crucified is seen as the Christ crucifying is the most serious missiological problem today in Asia. Is not this indeed a crucial issue for the life of the church? If this observation has any fragment of truth, may I say that our failure is not located in the periphery of the Christian faith but right at the vital heart of it. We have not been 'historical' enough to see what Christ crucified means to all of us in the different historical and cultural contexts. 'And go back to where you belong' does not solve the problem, although we must be thankful to Mr Leomala in pointing out for us the central issue in the Christian mission today. The presence of any possible suggestion to replace Christ crucified by Christ crucifying is against the foundation of the Christian understanding of history. Christianity failed to show 'respect' to history, and thus in the eyes of history it has become superficially historical.

Christianity is not identical with Jesus Christ. But Jesus Christ stands at the centre of Christianity. At the moment of our repentance we see him standing among us. 'Lo, I am with you always, to the close of the age.' This promise is the call for our repentance. In this promise Christianity has a future. The future belongs to those who repent. The content of repentance is 'Go therefore ... ' It is the movement of the crucified mind. As we repent, we begin to see our neighbours, their spirituality, their frustration, the aspiration to which Christ is ever speaking. *In repentance we become deeply historical.* Distance from repentance is distance from history. In repentance we see Jesus Christ crucified, not 'Christ crucifying'. 'The time is fulfilled, and the kingdom of God is at hand – repent and believe in the Gospel' (Mark 1.15).

10   The Risen Mind

The crucified mind is the Good-Friday-Easter mind and the
Easter-Good-Friday mind.

The relationship between human *ability* and human *lust*.

The risen mind believes in the possibility of the 'crucified-mind-
based crusading mind'.

Jesus Christ carries his cross – no handle on the cross!

The 'risen mind' is an awkward expression. By itself it is
unintelligible. It is the crucified mind which looks up to the
risen Lord.

The crucified Lord is the risen Lord. This is the foundation
of the apostolic preaching.

> For I delivered to you as of first importance what I also
> received, that Christ died for our sins in accordance with
> the scriptures, that he was buried, that he was raised on the
> third day in accordance with the scriptures and that he
> appeared to Cephas, then to the twelve' (I Cor. 15.3-5).
> ... Jesus Christ of Nazareth, whom you crucified, whom
> God raised from the dead ... (Acts 4.10).

On the way to a village named Emmaus the risen Jesus
drew near to two of the disciples. They gave him a complete
summary of the 'things that have happened there in these
days' (Luke 24.18).

> Concerning Jesus of Nazareth, who was a prophet mighty
> in deed and word before God and all the people, and how
> our chief priests and rulers delivered him up to be
> condemned to death, and crucified him. But we had hoped
> that he was the one to redeem Israel. Yes, and besides all
> this, it is now the third day since this happened. Moreover,
> some women of our company amazed us. They were at the
> tomb early in the morning and did not find his body; and

they came back saying that they had even seen a vision of angels, who said that he was alive. Some of those who were with us went to the tomb, and found it just as the women had said; but him they did not see' (vv.19-24).

Here is a soul-searching and painful expression of hope ending in disappointment. 'That very day' (v.13) of resurrection was being spent without the assurance of faith in the risen Lord. Jesus was crucified. They knew. But here is an empty tomb instead of the 'full tomb'. Now the women said that 'he was alive'. Yes. They set off for Emmaus. What for? What do they do when they get there with a profound experience of disappointment? Will they have something more than what the women told them? The stranger took up the subject of the talk. He told them that 'the Christ should suffer these things and enter into his glory' (v.26). In the evening the three sat at table in the village. ' ... he took the bread and blessed, and broke it, and gave it to them. And their eyes were opened and they recognized him; and he vanished out of their sight' (vv.30f.). Was not this gesture the same as he did 'on the night when he was betrayed' (I Cor. 11.23; Luke 22.14-23)? The meaning of the last supper, the arrest, the humiliation and crucifixion now became *one* saving story when he, the risen Lord, broke the bread again in Emmaus. 'Did not our hearts burn within us while he talked to us on the road ... ' (v.32).

Until Jesus 'took the bread and blessed and broke it' for the *second* time, his followers were left in a crisis of hopelessness and confusion. Chronology cannot contain the event of resurrection as paper cannot contain fire. The New Testament does not describe *how* Jesus was raised. The resurrection of Jesus Christ must be a new experience for time!

The crucified Lord was timed. 'It was now about the sixth hour ... Then Jesus, crying with a loud voice, said, "Father, into thy hands I commit my spirit"! And having said this he breathed his last' (Luke 23.44-46). He suffered under Pontius Pilate. 'On the third day' he rose from the dead. This is the day on which the ultimate mystery of the convenant God took place. Time must stop, since it does not know how to behave at this great mystery. When time stopped, the whole creation stopped. That is to say that the whole creation was brought into crisis in order to exist on the new quality of time henceforth. The risen Lord means, then, the coming of the new time, the new order, the new covenant and the new humanity. The risen mind is the mind that experienced this unusual disruption of time. It is the mind captivated by the presence of the new quality of time within this history of ours. It is, then, an extremely unusual mind which sees time in the light of Jesus Christ crucified and risen. It is the mind of faith. It works with the discernment of faith and sees what is not visible and believes what is impossible.

The risen mind is a *gift* which comes to us as we watch him as he 'took the bread and blessed and broke it ... ' *twice*, once before the crucifixion and once after the resurrection. These two tables are related. How can they be related when between them time was disrupted? Jesus Christ crucified and risen! The same Jesus Christ! He sat at the table twice for us. In him is found the vital cohesion. ' ... there is no Easter without Good Friday, but equally certainly there is no Good Friday without Easter!'[22] The risen mind is the crucified mind, the crucified mind is the risen mind. And the risen mind is the crucified mind captivated by the same Lord who sat twice at the table for us. It is the Good-Friday-Easter mind. It is the Easter-Good-Friday mind. It lives in that mystery of theological sequence.

> Death is swallowed up in victory O death, where is thy victory? O death, where is thy sting? The sting of death is sin, and the power of sin is the law. But thanks be to God, who gives us the victory through our Lord Jesus Christ. Therefore, my beloved brethren be steadfast, immovable, always abounding in the work of the Lord, knowing that in the Lord your labour is not in vain (I Cor. 15.54-58).

The risen mind lives in the promise of this ultimate victory.

Therefore (precisely as in the case of 'go therefore ... ') it is commanded by the apostle to be 'always abounding in the work of the Lord'. The risen mind is not a quietist mind. It is not an activist mind. It is 'always abounding in the work of the Lord' because it is guided by the experience gained at the two tables of the Lord. It is 'steadfast, immovable' in the way the crucified and risen Lord is. It is a resourceful mind *receiving* its resourcefulness from the Jesus Christ crucified and risen. Its resourcefulness is basically crucified-and-risen resourcefulness. It is that of faith, hope and love. It is not a self-generated resourcefulness. It is not afraid of meeting people of other living faiths. It is 'steadfast, immovable' with them, yet it knows how to conduct, with all sincerity, profitable 'table talks' with them since it has been in training at the table twice. It remembers the truth of the crucified Lord – the crucified truth – and how this truth should be communicated by self-denial. It respects history. It refused to 'handle' history.

I find in the speech which Martin Luther King gave at Mason Temple, Memphis, Tennessee on 3 April 1968 (the day before he was assassinated) for the rally to organize the sanitation workers in Memphis a resounding expression of the risen mind, the Good-Friday-Easter mind and the Easter-Good-Friday mind.

The first question that the Levite asked was, 'If I stop to help this man, what will happen to me?' But then the Good Samaritan came by. And he reversed the question. 'If I do not stop to help this man, what will happen to him?' That's the question before you tonight. ... Let us rise up tonight with a greater readiness. Let us stand with a greater determination. And let us move on, in these powerful days, these days of challenge, to make America what it ought to be. We have an opportunity to make America a better nation. And I want to praise God once more for allowing me to be here with you ... Well, I don't know what will happen now. We've got some difficult days ahead, but it really doesn't matter with me now because I've been to the

mountain top. And I don't mind. Like anybody, I would
like to live a long life. Longevity has its place. But I am not
concerned about that now. I just want to do God's will.
And He has allowed me to go up to the mountain. And I've
looked over, and I've seen the Promised Land. I may not get
there with you, but I want you to know tonight that we as a
people will get to the Promised Land. So I'm happy
tonight. I'm not worried about anything. I'm not fearing
any man. Mine eyes have seen the glory of the coming of the
Lord.[23]

In his mind Jesus Christ is the Good Samaritan who
reversed the question. Indeed, if it were not so how can we
make saving sense out of the Christian social practice? 'Let us
rise up tonight ... ' looking straight at the risen Lord whom
God raised from the dead. His call for mobilization is deeply
rooted in the call of God to new humanity. So his vision of the
new Memphis comes together with his vision of the Promised
Land. Memphis and the Promised Land are talked about in
the light of the experience of the 'two tables'. Against all
terrible odds he declares, 'I'm not fearing any man. Mine eyes
have seen the glory of the coming of the Lord.' The risen mind
glimpses the Promised Land. Because of this glimpse he is
powerful, resourceful, inspiring and energetic. Yet this
physical and spiritual power is an expression of his inner self-
denial. 'Longevity has its place. But I am not concerned about
that now. I just want to do God's will.' In his vision of a new
Memphis (the community of human dignity and social
justice) and his theologically structured joyous and hopeful
self-denial ('I just want to do God's will') he served his fellow
men, followed the Jesus Christ crucified and risen, and
worshipped his God.

'The sense of man', to use an expression of Teilhard de
Chardin, expressed itself movingly in Martin Luther King.

The nature of the sense of man is such that it brings men
closer together, and inspires them, in the expectation of a
future; in the certainty, that is to say, that something is

becoming a reality whose existence is not strictly
demonstrable but is nevertheless accepted with even more
assurance than demonstration and touch could afford. The
sense of man is a faith.

Its nature, again, is such that it subordinates the whole of
the activities for which it provides the basic directive force
to the preparation and service of this great thing whose
emergence is foreshadowed. The work now in progress in
the universe, the mysterious final issue in which we are
collaborating, is that 'great unit' which must take
precedence over everything, and to which everything must
be sacrificed, if success is to be ours. The sense of man is a
summons to renunciation.

Faith and renunciation – and what are those if not the
two attributes essential to all worship?[24]

I see in Martin Luther King faith and renunciation, neither
morbid nor arrogant, but joyous and healthy – which have,
according to the Jesuit seer of the twentieth century, a vast
cosmic significance. The far-reaching beauty of the mind
trained at the *table twice*! Faith and renunciation are the secret
of the Good-Friday-Easter mind and Easter-Good-Friday
mind.

What will the mind which sits twice at the table of the Lord
say of the 'high-protein lunch-box'? What does the risen mind
which is the crucified mind remembering the risen Lord (the
most 'resourceful' Lord!) say of the resourceful lunch-box? I
have indicated the possibility of renewal in human spirituality
when human resourcefulness is placed under the hope and
judgment of the crucified Lord. Let me briefly engage in a
further discussion on this issue as we come to the close of this
book.

' ... and behold, now I bring the first of the fruit of the
ground, which thou, O Lord, hast given me' is the way that
the first liturgical expression of the faith is concluded (Deut.
26.5-10). 'The fruit of the ground' in the twentieth century is
far more varied, plentiful and sophisticated than it was in the

time of ancient Israel. Civilization (with enlightened methods
applied to the increase and use of the 'fruit of the ground')
expresses itself at three principal points: language, tool and
fire. We are today living in the profusion of the spoken and
printed words, we use the most powerful advanced tools, and
we are in possession of the ultimate form of fire, nuclear
energy. We can think of 'the fruit of the ground' as
representing the entire substance of our civilization.

The prophet Hosea speaks of 'the fruit of the ground' in a
much more controversial context. 'And she did not know that
it was I who gave her the grain, the wine, and the oil, and who
lavished upon her silver and gold which they used for Baal'
(2.8). When the fruit of the ground is 'used for Baal', the
personification of the power of fertility, will it endanger the life
of man on this planet? Why is it critically urgent for man to
know that 'it was I' who gave 'the fruit of the ground'? What
difference does it make one way or the other? Is God jealous?
Is he simply after recognition?

Baal represents both human and cosmic fertility
(potentiality to increase). Since it is concerned with 'increase',
and not 'decrease', it is hopeful, positive, energetic and
productive. It is an expression of vitality. It contains the
principle of hard work. It has the mind of sharp calculation. In
Baal is the principle of development. Then why was Hosea
and the host of the other prophets so concerned about the
danger of Baal for the covenant people? Did not God himself
say 'Be fruitful and multiply' (Gen. 1.28)? Are we not in the
twentieth century intended to be hopeful, energetic,
productive and increase-minded?

The principle of Baal is not harmful to the human
community as long as it means simply the principle of
increase. But Baal does not stay this way. Baal becomes the
power of *lust* to increase ... used for lust'! It becomes the Gross
National Product drive instead of the Gross National Welfare
drive! Hitler's National Socialism mobilized 'the fruit of the
ground' lustfully to its demonic end. The Republic of South
Africa lustfully and resourcefully (down to every smallest

detail) maintains its racist *apartheid* policy. Japan has been quickly and substantially rearming herself – lust to increase – ignoring the post-Hiroshima-Nagasaki 'Peace New Constitution' (1946, 'Aspiring sincerely to an international peace based on justice and order, the Japanese people forever renounce war as a sovereign right of the nation and the threat or use of force as means of settling international disputes', Article 9).

The reason for our tragic human situation, sharply pointed out by the prophet of the eighth century BC, speaks straight to us with devastating inescapability. One of the important ecumenical discussions held in 1974 has this to say:

> At a time when 900 millions are malnourished and the human community is engaged on an economic and military course which could destroy all life upon this planet, Christians are called to a new witness and new actions to challenge the reckless exploitation of human beings by human beings and nature by humanity. During the last twenty years there has been a tendency to involve all human societies within this exploitative, GNP-oriented, world-wide system, sometimes even pursued in the name of God and humanity. We cannot hope to change humanity's relationship to nature without changing the relationship of men and women to each other. These changes call for the transformation of existing social orders, although the methods and details will differ according to the history, and circumstances of different societies. In all types of societies, affluent and poor, ancient and modern, large and small, human beings need to seek new life styles – styles which do not depend upon the escalation of economic growth involving the exhaustion of the earth's resources, destruction of the land, the sea and the air; styles which avoid large dehumanizing machines – like bureaucratic and industrial structures, which fragment communities and alienate human beings from God, from themselves and from each other.[25]

This situation has come about not by the *ability* to increase, but by the *lust* to increase. Baal grabs 'the grain ... ' Baal grabs 'the oil ... ' When man grabs 'the fruit of the ground', he is seized by lust to increase. He becomes dedicated to use the fruit of the ground for Baal! To say that Baal has given man 'the grain, the wine, and the oil, silver and gold' is to say, 'These are your gods, O Israel, who brought you up out of the land of Egypt' to the golden calves. At this wilful denial of the grace of the covenant God, that is to say, at this point of intentional destruction of the principle of honest covenant relationship between God and man, and man and man, *ability* changes into *lust*. When the covenant relationship is destroyed we find ourselves inescapably in the evil of a grabbing situation. The grabbing situation is an idolatrous situation. To be grabbing is to be idolatrous. When the chief tax officer Zacchaeus said 'Behold, Lord, the half of my goods I give to the poor; and if I have defrauded any one of anything (certainly he had) I restore it fourfold' (Luke 19.8) – these are words which we desperately need to hear from the chairman of the boards of the multi-national monster corporations! – he is freed from idolatry to the life of the covenant relationship. 'Today salvation has come to this house, since he also is a son of Abraham' (v.9). In a grabbing situation, *ability* changes into *lust*. Or rather, grabbing ability is called lust. In today's global language, lust is a sick ability to enjoy privately resourceful life in the face of 900 million famished people.

It is important, yes, critically important to know that ' ... it was I who gave her the grain ... '. It is this 'I' who comes to us *in no grabbing way* and renews our life by judging our 'lust to increase' (grab-ability). God asks the question: 'Where are you?' He seeks a continuous living relationship with the whole of humanity. He does not come to us with handle-mindedness. He rules history. He reorganizes history. He revives history. Finally, he gave himself to redeem history in his Son Jesus Christ. Jesus Christ was crucified (utter self-giving, self-denial). His hands are painfully neither open nor closed for all of us. His crucified hands proclaim his extraordinary 'yes' to our history. This is the 'I' of ' ... it was I who gave ... '.

We have characterized the image of the lunch-box as 'high-protein' human resourcefulness. This resourcefulness must be understood as a gift from God. Almost always in our human experience resourcefulness and handle-mindedness go together. The crusading mind consists of resourcefulness plus handle-mindedness. It is then in danger of 'handling' history. What we need is a crucified-mind-based crusading mind. It is the crusading mind with the painful hands neither open nor closed. *Such a crusading mind is not an ordinary concept of crusading mind. Crucified crusading mind! Crucified resourcefulness mind!* Here resourcefulness and handle-mindedness are separated! At the moment of this fission – fission between *ability* and *lust*, the Baal-mind and Yahweh-mind – our history experiences genuinely life-giving energy. This fission must take place wherever human resourcefulness is found. In situations of both 'crusade for ... ' and 'crusade against ... ', in both grave and less grave contexts, crusading mind must experience the explosive and incomparable energy of the one whose hands are painfully neither open nor closed. In such a theological context, the word 'crusade' or 'crusading' is no longer usable. The word is replete with the memory of tragic human limitation of vision, self-righteousness and arrogance. But that is not the most important issue involved here. What is at the centre of our concern is to look at human resourcefulness, however great or small, in the light of Jesus Christ, crucified and risen.

The apostolic preaching proclaims that Jesus Christ crucified is the victor! The risen Christ means the vindication of his life which culminated as he carried the handleless cross and was nailed to it. He suffered for us. He did not handle us. The mind that sits at the Lord's Table twice is inspired to believe in the 'efficacy' of the one who denied himself and carried the handleless cross to the end of history. 'Then Jesus told his disciples, "If any man would come after me, let him deny himself and take up his cross and follow me ... " '. 'Lo, I am with you always, to the close of the age' (Matt. 28.20).

Notes

1. *Ecumenical Sharing of Personnel Report*, World Council of Churches, Geneva, July 1972.
2. Ogbu U. Kalu, *International Review of Mission*, April 1975, p.146.
3. P.J. Skinner, quoted in *The Interpreter's Bible*, Vol.I, Abingdon Press, Nashville and New York 1952, p.564.
4. Gerhard von Rad, *Old Testament Theology*, Vol.1, SCM Press 1975 and Harper and Row, New York, p.163.
5. Joachim Wach, *Types of Religious Experience, Christian and Non-Christian*, University of Chicago Press 1951, p.43.
6. Mahatma Gandhi, *An Autobiography, The Story of My Experiments with Truth*, Luzac 1950, pp.123f.
7. K.M. Panikkar, *Asia and Western Dominance*, Allen and Unwin 1959, pp.26f.
8. Article 9, *The Lausanne Covenant*, 1974.
9. Karl Barth, *Church Dogmatics* I, 2, T. & T. Clark 1956, pp.302f.
10. Gerhard von Rad, *Old Testament Theology*, Vol.1, p.230.
11. Bernhard W. Anderson, *The Living World of the Old Testament*, Longmans 1967 (USA: *Understanding the Old Testament*, Prentice-Hall), p.315.
12. G. Quell, 'Agape', in *Theological Dictionary of the New Testament* I, Eerdmans, Grand Rapids 1964, p.32.
13. Kenneth Cragg, *The Call of the Minaret*, Oxford University Press 1956, p.42.
14. Frithjof Schuon, *Understanding Islam*, Allen and Unwin 1963, p.16.
15. *Bhagavadgita*, ch.xii, vv.13, 16, translated by S. Radhakrishnan.
16. Buddhadasa Bhikku, *Buddha Dhamma for Students*, Sublime Life Mission, Bangkok 1966, p.51.
17. *Selected Works of Mao Tse-Tung*, Vol.IV, Foreign Languages Press, Peking 1969, p.16.
18. B.D. Napier, *Exodus*, Laymans Bible Commentaries, SCM Press and John Knox Press, Atlanta 1963, p.30.
19. Gerhard von Rad, *Old Testament Theology*, Vol.2, SCM Press 1975 and Harper and Row, New York, pp.204, 206.
20. R.E. Brown, *The Gospel according to John*, The Anchor Bible, Doubleday, New York 1966 and Geoffrey Chapman 1971, pp.393f.
21. C. Peter Wagner, *International Review of Mission*, April 1975, p.174.
22. Karl Barth, *Dogmatics in Outline*, SCM Press 1949, p.114.
23. Dick Gregory, *No More Lies*, Harper and Row 1970, pp.342f., 345.
24. Pierre Teilhard de Chardin, *Towards the Future*, Collins and Harper and Row, New York 1975, p.23.
25. 'Report: Science and Technology for Human Development. The Ambiguous Future and the Christian Hope. 1974 World Conference in Bucharest', *Anticipation*, November 1974, p.17.